Praise For *Ed*

"Church innovation is hyper-local." I love this insight by my friend Josh Broward. And he is right. The church of Jesus begins by seeing the neighborhood through the eyes of Jesus, not by an entrepreneur who hijacks a people to fulfill her or his lust for doing something different. These stories give me hope for the church in North America. In my current role, I observe about 1,600 churches in their annual report gatherings. Some of the churches in this book are among these. I admire the pastors who love the people of their communities more than they love the novelty of their ideas. I vote yes for more *Edison Churches*.

Dan Boone
President, Eastern Nazarene College
President, Trevecca Nazarene University

Finally! A book about churches that embrace the counterintuitive truth of the kingdom of God: failure. Ours is a movement built on the most epic failure of all time—a crucified Messiah. Only those courageous communities who follow in this way will discover the breakthroughs of resurrection. It will take *Edison Churches* to light the way.

J.D. Walt
Vice President, Seedbed
Asbury Theological Seminary

Good news: God still works through the agency of the church to proclaim in word and deed the gospel of Jesus Christ. But it is painfully apparent that the forms and structures that have served the church in the West so well for the past couple centuries are, in many cases, faltering. Most of us are aware that we need new expressions of the church that are true to the gospel as well as relevant to the cultural context. We need new wineskins! That's why I'm so impressed with *Edison Churches*, which is a well-written, timely, and urgently needed book that offers examples of innovative expressions of the church in a variety of contexts. I highly recommend *Edison Churches* to pastors and lay leaders who are willing to think creatively as they consider the life and witness of the church in new ways.

Ron Benefiel
Center for Pastoral Leadership
Point Loma Nazarene University

You may be offended when you read *Edison Churches*—and that's not bad. It approaches the very personal experience of longing to do something big and frequently failing. But the authors help us recast our illusionary love affair with success. This book will open your eyes to see the fullness of truly leaning into a radical, risk-taking, edgy posture of being kingdom churches in meaningful and impactful ways.

Kevin Mannoia
Professor of Ministry and Chaplain, Azusa Pacific University
Founder and Chair, Wesleyan Holiness Consortium

In the twenty-first century—and particularly in increasingly post-Christian environments—the church must face the need for innovation. With innovation comes the risk and reality of failure. Simply put, life together as followers of Christ is risky business because of the scandal of a crucified Savior, yet we too often strive in the church for security, strength, and stability. These adjectives do not coincide with the volatile situations in which the gospel is birthed and expressed. *Edison Churches* challenges the church back to its roots—that is, the great risk that following in faith requires. In new times and places, the church as a living organism must break out of stable molds to be a movement that expresses the kingdom anew. This book offers lived examples of how communities of Christ followers are doing just that.

Nell Becker Sweeden
Director, Nazarene Compassionate Ministries
Global Ministry Center for the Church of the Nazarene

If you only take one thought from *Edison Churches,* it should be that failure can be a good thing! The freedom to fail is a vital and necessary ingredient of innovation. Read about the fascinating churches the book describes and see how the willingness to dream, experiment, dare, and—sometimes—fail can be the process God uses to help us discover beautiful new ways of being the church. I will buy *Edison Churches* for every pastor on our district.

Rick Power
District Superintendent
Hawaii-Pacific District, Church of the Nazarene

God is doing a new thing—actually, new *things.* The prime exhibits of this divine novelty are the diverse, provocative, and sometimes plain *weird* new churches that are emerging. *Edison Churches* inspires us to explore fresh and zesty ways to live as Jesus communities in our time.

Thomas Jay Oord
Co-author, *Relational Holiness*
Co-editor, *Renovating Holiness*

It's probably been a while since you read any kind of book that begins with these words: "We need to fail more. Churches need to fail more. Leaders need to fail more." But this one does, and for good reason. We focus too much on leadership and not enough on followership. Followers learn from failure. They grow from it, and they are better for it. But it requires that they follow the right things—or, rather, the right Person. *Edison Churches* is about churches that seek to imitate Christ in all of his servanthood, all of his going to the margins, all of his suffering—in other words, all of the things the world considers *failure*—and, in doing so, proves once again that the call of Christ leads our churches to the true kingdom.

Bruce Barnard
Lead Pastor, Mission New York
Director of Operations, Metro NY District, Church of the Nazarene

Here at last is a book of fundamental information on innovative churches that have risked getting out of their comfort zones with the Edison-like commitment to advance the kingdom of God in their surrounding communities and beyond. In *Edison Churches*, you will find the essence of missional churches and, most importantly, be inspired to participate in God's mission in proactive and innovative ways.

Musung Jung
Assistant Professor of Missiology
Korea Nazarene University

If you have ever pastored a church, then you are more than likely familiar with the phrase "We've never done it like that before." It's the mantra that keeps the status quo strong and those who want to change it at bay. Sadly, innovation in churches can be difficult. Innovation faces opposition from both leaders and followers. *Edison Churches* refreshingly encourages new ways of embracing Christ in an ever-changing world. I was empowered reading the stories of churches that faced the tired mantra and offered something different, something new, something courageous.

Padraic Ingle
Lead Pastor
Faith Community Church of the Nazarene

While guarding the gospel *message*, John Wesley dared to experiment with the *method* in order to reach the neglected and forgotten of eighteenth-century England. The same kind of holy boldness shines through *Edison Churches* in ten compelling, twenty-first-century stories. The lessons these Spirit-led innovators learned will spark fruitful discussion and action in any church that hungers to move from the status quo to God's something better.

Gregory Crofford, PhD
Dean, School of Religion and Christian Ministry
Africa Nazarene University

At a time when there is much evidence of church decline in the West, the authors of *Edison Churches* have pulled together inspiring stories of innovation and breakthrough from churches across the U.S. and Europe. They identify key principles and practices that allow churches to thrive and multiply in ways that defy cultural expectations. This book will encourage, inspire, and motivate you to take risks as you seek to follow Jesus into kingdom breakthrough.

Paul Maconochie
Global Leader, 3D Movements
Former Pastor, St. Thomas Crookes Anglican Church

3

Edison Churches

Experiments in Innovation and Breakthrough

Jesse C. Middendorf
Megan M. Pardue

Greg Arthur
Josh Broward

THE FOUNDRY
PUBLISHING

Copyright © 2017 by Beacon Hill Press of Kansas City
Beacon Hill Press of Kansas City
PO Box 419527
Kansas City, MO 64141
beaconhillbooks.com

978-0-8341-3670-0

Printed in the
United States of America

Cover designer: Arthur Cherry
Interior designer: Sharon Page

Library of Congress Cataloging-in-Publication Data
Names: Middendorf, Jesse C., author.
Title: Edison churches : experiments in innovation and breakthrough /
    Jesse Middendorf, Megan M. Pardue, Greg Arthur, Josh Broward.
Description: Kansas City, MO : Beacon Hill Press of Kansas City, 2017. |
    Includes bibliographical references.
Identifiers: LCCN 2017034548 | ISBN 9780834136700 (pbk.)
Subjects: LCSH: Church renewal—Case studies. | Failure   (Psychology)—
    Religious aspects—Christianity—Case studies. | Christianity—21st century.
Classification: LCC BV600.3 .E37 2017 | DDC 262.001/7—dc23 LC record available at
    https://lccn.loc.gov/2017034548

The internet addresses, email addresses, and phone numbers in this book are
accurate at the time of publication. They are provided as a resource. Beacon
Hill Press of Kansas City does not endorse them or vouch for their content or
permanence.

10 9 8 7 6 5 4 3 2 1

Table of Contents

Foreword

A NUMBER of years ago I was walking through the ruins of Ephesus, listening to the guide tell us of the remarkable Greek and Roman cultures. The engineering accomplishments were simply amazing—some of their secrets have yet to be unlocked. In a moment of admiration, the guide took a deep breath and said, "If only they had discovered electricity!" The reality is that electricity would have elevated ancient culture to levels unknown.

Throughout history, there are moments and events that will define the future. Thomas Edison spent much of his life exploring electricity and its uses, which ushered in a new era in which everything we had previously taken for granted suddenly changed. Thomas Friedman's book *Thank You for Being Late* challenges us to think critically about the ever-changing and dynamic world in which we live. Much of the change in our world has to do with the way technology has become a vital link to all of our lives. Technological advances have always had a profound effect upon society. Specifically, Edison's advances with electricity completely transformed society as we knew it.

In 2017, we are celebrating the 500th anniversary of the Christian Reformation. Many would ask whether the Reformation would have been possible if not for the invention of the printing press. Suddenly, the Bible could be printed and placed into the hands of many people—and everything changed. Theological treatises and documents spread throughout the land. Even though the printing press brought great change, the pace at which these changes were absorbed into society was actually rather slow and steady. The printing press was improved and enhanced throughout the centuries, but it was not completely transformed until the digital age. Only in the past fifteen years have printed books, newspapers, and magazines been slowly replaced by digital reading devices. For 500 years, we were able to slowly adapt. Times of change were often followed by a static state in which everyone could adjust and relax until the next change occurred.

We no longer live in that world. According to Friedman, "The rate of technological change is now accelerating so fast that it has risen above the average rate at which most people can absorb all these changes. Many of us cannot keep pace anymore." He goes on to say, "Indeed, there is a mismatch between the change in the pace of change and our ability to develop the learning systems, training systems, management systems, social safety nets, and government regulations that would enable citizens to get the most out of these accelerations and cushion their worst impacts."[1] This is, in effect, the contemporary world of Edison: a new world, rapid change, and ideas that need to interface with the complexities of transformation.

All of these changes have an impact on the church and how we will plant churches and minister in the future. These changes are also why we can't spend too much time looking back but must keep looking forward. While we used to be able to take time to adjust to change and enjoy the static state, we now must acknowledge and accept that we will remain constantly in motion. Life, work, and ministry will be dynamic, and we must become accustomed to doing our work while we are on the move. Hence, *Edison Churches*.

We are told that enhancing our ability to adapt is "90 percent about 'optimizing for learning'—applying features that drive technological innovation to our culture and social structures. Every institution, whether it is the patent office, which has improved a lot in recent years, or any other major government regulatory body, has to keep getting more agile —it has to be willing to experiment quickly and learn from mistakes."[2] Friedman also tells us, "Universities are now experimenting with turning over their curriculum much faster and more often to keep up with the change in the pace of change—putting a 'use-by date' on certain courses."[3] For the church, this means we need to be adaptable in terms of our methodologies, but we also need to remain grounded in eternal truths.

While the world becomes weary from change, the church can become a place of respite. It may be for this very reason that traditional worship is attractive for some individuals. There is an anchor here that ties us to the past and doesn't feel as if it is ready to spin off the flywheel. We may be surprised to learn that older forms of worship have become appealing to younger people who feel overwhelmed by the rapid pace of change. At the same time, Edison churches take a number of approaches when it comes to contextualizing ministry. Everyone needs to begin thinking like a missionary and adapting to the changing world so the good news of the gospel can continue to transform lives.

Before we jump in and decide we want to adopt a particular model for change, I would suggest a word of caution. We will always have to be talking about change. We have entered a new, dynamic era in which we will no longer be looking to arrive at *the* answer for the church. Instead, we look to our guiding principles to keep us on a path in which we remain faithful as we work within this fluid and dynamic environment. There is something spiritual to be found here. Edison churches must be open to the continual and ongoing movement of God's Holy Spirit. There must be space for the wind to blow. The beauty is that, when everything feels so out of control, we may just discover the peace and comfort that are found in radically trusting God.

Carla Sunberg
General Superintendent
Church of the Nazarene

1
Embracing Failure

WE NEED TO FAIL. Churches need to fail more. Leaders need to fail more. Pharmaceutical giant Eli Lilly has, since the 1990s, been hosting what he calls failure parties for scrapped research projects.[1] Edgy design company 5Crowd has a failure party every month—complete with failure high-fives and often wrapping up with a celebratory failure cake![2] When venture capitalists assess whether to invest in a new idea, one of the key characteristics they look for is a previous failed startup. They prefer to invest in a leader who has already run a company into the ground.[3]

Entrepreneurs in one of America's most embattled cities have gathered under the unlikely banner of Fail Detroit. They convene monthly to share their stories of failures and missteps for mutual edification and encouragement.[4] Fail Faire is a movement of conferences dedicated to cultivating space for people to share their greatest failures. Started by nonprofit Mobile Active and promoted by World Bank, the idea is such a hit that it has been duplicated around the world in places as far flung as Singapore, Kenya, Canada, and California. The simple appeal is a place "where it's okay to talk about failing."[5]

Best of all, there's an entire publication specifically dedicated to documenting "humankind's boldest missteps." *Failure* magazine shares stories of spectacular bombs from sports, arts, science, and business. The editors cheekily explain: "Failure: It's an option."[6] Consulting company Fail Forward boasts their ability to help their clients "fail intelligently," and they define intelligent failure as "the practice of smart risk taking and maximizing learning."[7]

Why All the Fuss about Failure?

"Not all failures are created equal," argues Harvard professor Amy Edmondson. She goes on to explain that there are failures of performance, failures of context, and failures of experiment.[8] We can learn from all of them, but the third category—failures of experiment—is the gold mine.

"Failure can actually be a huge engine of innovation for an individual or an organization," explains Baba Shiv of the Stanford Graduate School of Business. "The trick lies in approaching it with the right attitude and harnessing it as a blessing, not a curse."[9]

—◊◊◊—

> **Let's remove the stigma we've attached to**
> **failure and talk about it openly. We can learn**
> **and grow from our failings—but only if**
> **we're not constantly hiding them.**

—◊◊◊—

Failure is absolutely crucial to breakthrough success. Overcoming longstanding barriers requires creativity, innovation, and experimentation. The key for organizations is to develop cultures that encourage the broad experimentation that is necessary to fumble forward toward successful new models, ideas, and practices.

We are in an era of rapid and discontinuous change. The rapid explosion of technological innovation has caused a chain reaction of exponential change in every facet of human existence. We live in the Disruptive Century, according to *Fortune* magazine editor Alan Murray: "The question for the 21st century is, Who will allow the social and economic disruption that innovation brings? . . . Creative destruction threatens to clear away the business world we are familiar with to make way for one we aren't. The 21st century will belong to those who embrace that disruption rather than fight it."[10] In the midst of this shifting landscape of "creative destruction," the same old ways of operation are glaringly ineffective. Businesses that don't innovate are being swept into the dustbins of history. Churches that don't innovate are not far behind. And yet, innovation involves the nasty reality of failure.

Why Is Failure So Hard?

In 2011, *Harvard Business Review* dedicated an entire issue to failure. The editors explain: "Failure. We're hypocrites about it. Go online, and you'll find scores of pleasant aphorisms celebrating the inevitability of failure and the importance of learning from it. But in real life . . . failure is anathema. We're afraid of it. We avoid it. We penalize it. It's time for managers to get past platitudes and confront the F-word taboo."[11]

Let's be honest. Most of us hate failure. We hate to see our projects bite the dust. It cuts deep into our self-esteem and sense of identity. It can weaken our leadership capital and even threaten our careers. But the reality is that failure is inevitable. Everybody fails sometimes. For lots of reasons, in lots of ways, in many contexts, with and without fault, sometimes our best efforts just aren't enough. Let's remove the stigma we've attached to failure and talk about it openly. We can learn and grow from our failings—but only if we're not constantly hiding them.

In this era of immense change, we in the church need to get over our failure complex and begin to experiment more freely. We seem to have reached the limits of the church-growth attractional model. Bigger, better churches will still win some, but they will increasingly leave uninterested millions on the outside not even looking in. We must explore new ways to be the church in our new world. Jesus calls us out into deeper waters to fish for people in new ways, to plant the seeds of the kingdom in new soil, and to work for redemption while juggling both risk and opportunity.

—⁓—

In this era of immense change, we in the church need to get over our failure complex and begin to experiment more freely.

—⁓—

15

Our World Needs a New Church

Our world is radically different from the world our parents and grandparents grew up in, and it's becoming more different all the time. Our new world needs a new kind of church—but we don't know exactly what kind of church our world needs or how to become that kind of church. Our world has changed so dramatically that we must become missiologists within our own culture. Like missionaries encountering a brand-new people group, we must learn to study the language, customs, and thought patterns that structure our society. As we begin to understand our context anew, we can begin to imagine what a healthy, indigenous church will look like here in this place, with these people. But learning a culture takes time—decades, really—and we can't wait that long to start making changes. Our world needs a new church now, and we're the only church available.

Some brave pioneers have begun experimenting around the edges of church, spinning off different variations of Christian communities, birthing unique expressions of gospel-bearing, kingdom people. Sometimes it works, and sometimes it doesn't. But with each success and failure, we inch closer to a universal church that communicates and embodies the gospel in a way that is good news for our neighbors.

Edison Churches

One of the most easily recognizable examples of failure that leads to innovation may very well be glowing above your head as you read this. Few innovations have had the effect of changing our world quite like the spread of electricity and the commercial viability of the light bulb. The man primarily responsible for both of these innovations was, of course, Thomas Edison. Edison built an engineering empire that changed the way we live in fundamental ways. As a great inventor, he created a company that specialized in experimentation and failure.

Edison wasn't the only person to invent a light bulb. His company, however, was the first to create a commercially viable, reproducible, affordable bulb. He also pioneered the creation of an electric grid that would support his light bulb. No one, including Edison himself, really knew how many experiments and failures it took to create his light bulb. In an interview with *Harper's Monthly* magazine, Edison once explained: "I speak without exaggeration when I say that I have constructed three thousand different theories in connection with the electric light, each one of them reasonable and apparently true. Yet only in two cases did my experiments prove the truth of my theory."[12]

The simple light bulb—this world-changing innovation—required a radical commitment to thinking, experimenting, and learning from failure. We never know how long breakthrough will take or how many failures will come before success. Yet, without a commitment to innovation, we will certainly never experience breakthrough.

The crisis of the church in North America requires an Edison-like commitment. We need innovators who are unafraid of failure and will help us pioneer new ways of being the church in the twenty-first century. In this book, we'll look at ten innovative, future-leaning *Edison Churches*. These churches are wonderful examples of pioneers whose refusal to be afraid to fail led to innovation and breakthrough. They have paid the price of failure in pursuit of birthing a new future for the church. They are a diverse collection of churches from several theological tribes, multiple countries, and vastly differing contexts. We will share stories of church plants, historic churches, mega-churches, and everything in between.

These are stories of men and women, pastors and laypeople, who have bravely invested in the future of the church. We hope their stories will inspire a new generation of innovators who are willing to fail for the kingdom of God. You may not sell everything, or start a stripper ministry, or host potlucks for refugees. There is a good chance none of those ministry concepts will work in your particular context. Nonetheless, may we all be spurred to action by these adventurers who have allowed God's Spirit to birth something unique and beautiful in their own contexts. May we discover, together, a radical rebirth of the twenty-first-century church through this process of failure, innovation, and breakthrough.

In order to innovate, however, we must first understand where innovators come from and how God has hardwired innovation into the very DNA of the church. The church as we know it—spread across the globe, dominated by complicated infrastructures, birthed from empires, and having a seat at tables of power—is not the church that began in Jerusalem two thousand years ago. From the very beginning, God built the church as an ever-growing organism spreading out to the ends of the earth. From the very beginning, the mission was to move out from Jerusalem, planting the kingdom in new places. This work was led by innovators who were empowered by the Spirit of God. Somewhere along the way, as the church gained power, money, buildings, and institutions, we lost most of our pioneers and innovators. To go forward, we must first go backward and understand who God created us to be.

2

A Love Letter to Pioneers

Pioneer (noun)
1. A person or group that originates or helps open up a new line of thought or activity or a new method or technical development
2. One of the first to settle in a territory
3. A plant or animal capable of establishing itself in a bare, barren, or open area and initiating an ecological cycle

PIONEERS CAPTURE our imaginations in powerful ways. They are an elusive breed of people, seemingly detached from normal society. Confident in their skills, they step into the unknown to chase after glory, social advancement, or improved living conditions. Driven by their gut instinct toward the rewards they believe to be out there, these pioneers battle numerous setbacks and boldly confront the uncertain future. For the lucky ones, that future is indeed glorious, and their accomplishments are retold for generations to come. Brave, desperate, and a little bit crazy, these individuals are outliers. They are the exception to the rule. Why would anyone in their right mind leave behind familiar comforts to risk everything in pursuit of a dream? Certainly there are rewards to be had, but the cost is so high.

Even so, we love pioneers. We love wilderness adventurers who return with amazing, hard-to-believe stories. We revere obsessed geniuses working in their garages to create new technologies. We adore scientists who stay up all night or sleep in their labs, searching for the answers that will save humanity. We idolize astronauts, marveling at their willingness to leave this very planet to chase the great unknown. We love these people, but most of us don't want to be them. Stories, movies, or a good book about pioneers are plenty for most of us. We tend to believe that only the most extreme, desperate, courageous, intelligent, or heroic among us could ever be pioneers.

Pioneers of Faith

In the church, we have our own set of celebrated pioneers. Each tribe in the church has their heroes. Martin Luther, John Calvin, St. Francis, John Wesley, Francis Asbury, William Seymour, Phineas Bresee, William and Evangeline Booth, Mother Teresa—all are lauded for their pioneering kingdom work. Heroes inspire us! We rejoice in all they accomplished. They show up in our sermons. We build them statues and name movements after them. The heroes of our faith are the reasons our movements exist. We continue their work, inspired by the passion and vision they unleashed upon the world.

But having heroes can also weaken our movements. Our heroes are often our biggest obstacles to overcome in the pursuit of our calling. Reverence for our heroes has a counterintuitive effect on us. Instead of helping us, our heroes trap us. We become dependent on and subservient to their work. Hero worship reinforces our belief about the rare and extreme nature of pioneers. We celebrate these greats throughout history as a way of distancing ourselves from the work they did. They went into new places, carrying forth the work of God—so that we don't have to.

We are still living off the work of our pioneering heroes. They traveled to new lands for us. They started movements that reshaped the globe. Breaking through the limits of expectations and institutionalism, they cultivated new kingdom life in places where it previously had not reached. What have *we* done? On one hand, we've continued their work by growing the movements they began. On the other hand, we have also rebuilt institutional boundaries and limitations that closely resemble the structures these pioneers had to overcome in the first place. We fantasize about pioneers from a distance, but in practice, we are lovers of stasis.

We are paralyzed by the comforts of a world in which we claim God only calls the exceptional to pioneering work. None of us will have statues or movements named after us—and we are perfectly fine with that.

Take, for example, the incredible work of Francis Asbury. As an itinerant British pastor working in the colonies and then the newly formed United States, he took pioneering seriously. In a day when travel was difficult and slow, Asbury traveled more than 6,000 miles a year across the expanding frontier of North America. In his lifetime, he traveled more than 270,000 miles. During his four decades of ministry, the Methodist Episcopal Church grew from under 500 members to more than 210,000 members. He preached tens of thousands of sermons and devoted his life to the expansion and growth of the church.[1]

Asbury's influence and legacy are so deeply woven into American Methodism that they cannot be escaped. Schools bear his name. Millions of Methodists trace their heritage directly back to his work for the kingdom. There are statues of him—even one in Washington, DC. His work had such an effect on the expansion of our country that he is part of American history, not just church history.

How does hearing about Francis Asbury affect you? Does it amaze you? Do you marvel that anyone could live such a life? Do you feel connected to his work or distant from it? Most of us, when considering such an amazing pioneer, are certain we have never been called to that kind of life. The extraordinary makes the ordinary even more ordinary. We can't be Francis Asbury—right? Or can we?

Considering the stories of Asbury and other Christian pioneers, missiologist Alan Hirsch writes, "These are dangerous stories because they will subvert us into a journey that will call us to a more radical expression of Christianity than the one we currently experience."[2] What if God actually wants all our churches to be filled with pioneers? What if our assumptions on pioneer qualifications are entirely misconstrued? What if the spirit of pioneering is actually woven into the DNA of the church?

We may not all be equipped or called to start new movements, but the church was created to reproduce itself continually. We are not merely inheritors of a great legacy handed down by the heroes of our faith. The church, everywhere, at all times, is the living, breathing presence of God in the world. Imagine a church in which there was an expectation that each of us had a role in bringing life to new places. Imagine if we truly believed we were filled with the same power and presence of Christ that Francis Asbury exhibited. If that were true, there would be no need for statues to memorialize lone heroes. Instead of a people looking backward to admire the work of our predecessors, we would be a people whose best days are always in front of us.

—⁀—

We may not all be equipped or called to start new movements, but the church was created to reproduce itself continually.

—⁀—

Remembering our Reproductive DNA

The work of pioneering is intentionally woven into the DNA of the church. Alan Hirsch calls this the "apostolic genius" of the church.[3] It isn't actually that special. Wherever the Spirit of God is present in the life of the church, there too will be the call, ability, and power to pioneer.

A basic understanding of biology demonstrates that a healthy organism reproduces itself. When an organism stops reproducing, it goes extinct. The church, when healthy, will reproduce itself. The image Jesus used for this reproduction was that of a seed; after it grows, it produces a crop a hundred or a thousand times itself.

Why do we swap out Jesus's image of a seed, which reproduces itself regularly and with exponential growth, for that of a whale? The blue whale reproduces about once every two to three years, following a full, twelve-month gestation. Perhaps that rate of reproduction in the church is still too fast and fertile to be accurate. Better yet may be the image of a mule. Mules are the result of the pioneering, reproductive adventures of a horse and a donkey. They are a marvelously hybrid creation. Possessing a better disposition, a longer life span, and a more varied skill set than their parents, mules are remarkable creatures. The downside, however, is that mules are almost never fertile. While mules do on very rare occasions reproduce, it is exceptionally uncommon. It is so uncommon that, surely, other mules marvel at the impressive members of their breed who achieve it. They probably sing songs about them, name schools after them, and collect trading cards with their pictures on them.

The church is created to reproduce. A normal function of the shared mission and life of the followers of Christ is seeking opportunities to bring forth new life in Christ. Does this picture of the church seem foreign to us? Does it exist in a world we've never known? If so, we need to reimagine ourselves and rediscover our identity as pioneers because, somehow, our churches have ceased to be churchlike. The church was birthed in a wild explosion of God's dynamism in the lives of everyday people. The Spirit empowered an uncontrollable wildfire that wasn't limited by ethnicity, socioeconomic status, language, culture, geography, or religion. It was beautifully organic and full of life. Why, then, do our churches so seldom share these characteristics with the movement Jesus started?

Business expert Gary Hamel helpfully describes a similar problem in many companies: "There seems to be something in modern organizations that depletes the natural resilience and creativity of human beings, something that literally leeches these qualities out of employees during daylight hours. The culprit? Management principles and processes that foster discipline, punctuality, economy, rationality, and order yet place little value on artistry, nonconformity, originality, audacity, and elan. To put it simply, most companies are only fractionally human because they make room for only a fraction of the qualities and capabilities that make us human."[4]

Inhuman companies made up of humans are deeply similar to impotent churches made up with people filled with the creative power of God. In the same ways, our churches have learned to be efficient, organized, orderly, and effective at protecting and enforcing stasis. But efficiency, organization, and orderly conduct are not the primary goals of the church. The body of Christ should actually resemble Christ. It should defy expectations, resist institutional religion's efforts to control it, and subversively reproduce itself in an effort to change the world.

Bringing Life to Barren Lands

If we are to recover our pioneer identity, we need to go back to the basics. What is the mission of the church? Why do we exist? Naturally, the commission Jesus gave his disciples offers the answer to this question: "All authority in heaven and on earth has been given to me. Therefore go and make disciples of all nations, baptizing them in the name of the Father and of the Son and of the Holy Spirit, and teaching them to obey everything I have commanded you. And surely I am with you always, to the very end of the age" (Matthew 28:18–20).

Jesus commissioned his disciples to do something he himself did not do. He instructed them to go out into all nations to reproduce themselves. The disciples were now the rabbis. Jesus empowered his followers

23

with the authority to transition from being children to becoming parents. Filled with the same power and authority as Jesus, they went to new places and proclaimed the good news of Jesus. Accompanied by the power of God, this proclamation produced a harvest truly extraordinary in its magnitude. The basis of this commission is rooted in the beginning and end of Jesus's statement. First, he has been given all authority. There is no land where the disciples could go that would be outside the rule of Jesus. In addition, Jesus promised to be present with them wherever they went for as long as they went. As the inheritors of this Great Commission, its mission and its inherent promises are our spiritual legacy too. In all places, in all times, among all peoples—Jesus rules with power and authority. No matter where we go, Jesus is with us. Thus, we are a sent people, filled with power and a clear call to go reproduce the work of God in us.

Intrinsic to being a follower of Christ is the calling to go and to produce a new harvest for the kingdom as we go. At the moment of the Great Commission, the movement of Jesus consisted of a handful of uneducated Jews in the armpit of the Roman Empire. As the disciples looked out into the world around them, all they could see was barren land that had never had the seed of the gospel planted in it. Even so, this was the work God had long promised the Spirit would bring about. The church would go forth and bring life to barren lands. This is what a pioneering organism does. Of all the definitions of pioneer, the one that best fits the church is this: "a plant or animal [or organization, in our case] capable of establishing itself in a bare, barren, or open area and initiating an ecological cycle." Imagery of barren lands, wilderness, and the desert bursting forth with life is found throughout the Bible. One sure sign that the favor of God has come upon the earth is that places long uninhabited, lands long dormant, and cities that lie in ruins will flourish. Our God is a God who lives to breathe life into new places:

The desert and the parched land will be glad;
the wilderness will rejoice and blossom.
Like the crocus, it will burst into bloom;
it will rejoice greatly and shout for joy.
The glory of Lebanon will be given to it,
the splendor of Carmel and Sharon;
they will see the glory of the LORD,
the splendor of our God.

Strengthen the feeble hands,
steady the knees that give way;
say to those with fearful hearts,
"Be strong, do not fear;
your God will come,
he will come with vengeance;
with divine retribution
he will come to save you."
Then will the eyes of the blind be opened
and the ears of the deaf unstopped.
Then will the lame leap like a deer,
and the mute tongue shout for joy.
Water will gush forth in the wilderness
and streams in the desert.
The burning sand will become a pool,
the thirsty ground bubbling springs.
In the haunts where jackals once lay,
grass and reeds and papyrus will grow.
And a highway will be there;
it will be called the Way of Holiness;
it will be for those who walk on that Way.
Isaiah 35:1–8

God, who breathed life into dirt to give us life, is a God who loves to bring new life to barren places. It makes sense, then, that God has equipped the church to take up this work and join in the creative act of bringing forth new life. With the coming of the Holy Spirit at Pentecost, the church is launched out into barren land to pioneer new methods of discipleship. Lands that lie dormant, awaiting new life, burst forth in an array of God's abundance. The disciples began the work, but after Pentecost everyone in the early church pioneered in one way or another. Living as God's people, filled with God's Spirit, normal, everyday people suddenly became sowers of new life. Like an invasive plant, the church spread quickly throughout Jerusalem and the surrounding Jewish lands, and then, within a couple of decades, it had spread throughout the far-flung outposts of the Roman Empire.

The DNA of the church includes a fertility that catalyzes growth wherever the church flourishes. This fertility and growth are written into the blessing that Jesus gave his disciples in Acts 1:8: "But you will receive power when the Holy Spirit comes on you; and you will be my witnesses in Jerusalem, and in all Judea and Samaria, and to the ends of the earth." Any time the church is trapped in stasis, without reproduction, something is wrong.

If, then, this is the mission we are called to and the DNA of our rebirth, why don't we see more pioneering happening in the church? Why is the church in North America in a perpetual state of decline? Why do so few millennials (and even fewer in generation Z) find the church to be relevant to their lives? Why is the percentage of Americans who are uninterested in organized religion rapidly increasing? The reasons are legion—the long-term effects of the church functioning as an empire for a thousand years; the loss of a robust theology and practice of the presence of the Holy Spirit; the divide between clergy and laity; the separation of service and evangelism; and material affluence are all frequently cited as roots of our joint crisis. Scholarly and popular works sprout like dandelions to explain these reasons and their roots.

Nevertheless, what will it take for us to recover our reproductive mission and power? How can the church move from stasis back to growth? Can we rediscover our ability to pioneer, bringing life to barren lands?

Playing in the Dirt and Planning for Failure

"A great deal more failure is the result of an excess of caution than of bold experimentation with new ideas," argues J. Oswald Sanders. "The frontiers of the kingdom of God were never advanced by men and women of caution."[5] If we are to plant the seeds of good news into new lands once again, we must become cultivators. In Jesus's parable about the four soils (see Matthew 13:1–23), we can see clearly the difference cultivation makes in a seed's ability to be fruitful. The path trampled down was far too hard for any seed to take root. Sowing seed there was just feeding the birds. The rocky soil allowed a small bit of growth but nothing that would last over time. The weedy soil was great soil. Lots of things grew there. But no one took the time to remove the weeds, so the good seed was choked out. The good soil, however, was well tended and produced a huge harvest. Pioneering requires quite a bit of cultivating.

There are beautiful and blessed occasions when we stumble into well-cultivated land just waiting for good news to be planted. When we find that rich soil, waiting on new life, we rejoice in the goodness of God. We plant, we water, we watch the harvest grow, and we reap the harvest. Thanks be to God! In the 1990s, the Church of the Nazarene stumbled upon some good soil. At the time, there were zero Nazarenes in Bangladesh. But God connected the church with one Christian who would be our pioneer in a nation of Muslims and Hindus. The Church of the Nazarene organized its first congregation in 1995 with only a few dozen members. More than two decades later, there are 2,500 organized churches and more than 100,000 Nazarenes in Bangladesh. There is no rational explanation for this incredible kingdom harvest in such a short time aside from good seed, good soil, and good farming.

On the other hand, during that same time frame, church attendance in the United States dropped by more than 12 percent—around 4,000 churches a year closed their doors. Young people are dropping out of church left and right, and some 44 percent of the American population is now classified as post-Christian.

Sit with this painful comparison for a moment. In a predominantly Muslim country, a brand-new church pioneered a kingdom work that saw thousands of new churches organized in two decades. Meanwhile, in a country where religious freedoms are legally protected, many denominations—with thousands of paid clergy, vast resources, hundreds of thousands of members, and beautiful buildings—saw a decline in their numbers across the board. It's a bit like being an unsuccessful lifetime golfer and watching video of a five-year-old child hit a hole-in-one. You've worked your whole life and have never achieved what someone just starting out has already achieved.

The church in North America is filled with many of us who are desperate for new answers because we are working hard, we are educated, we are leveraging all the resources we have—and it still isn't working. We are righteously hungry for a harvest to spring forth from the land we are working. Clearly, some soils need a lot more cultivating than others. So how do we begin?

Step one is learning the land. Context is king when trying to grow something. If you don't have the answers to basic questions, you probably won't be successful over the long haul. What is the soil like? What grows there? What is the weather like? What are the dry and wet seasons? How long is the growing season? Where is the water source? What barriers are in the soil? Before you try to bring about a harvest, you have to pay close attention to the land. To be good farmers of the kingdom seed, we must engage a life of patient, intentional cultivation.

Pioneering new life is an act of innovation. It is a commitment to failure, over and over again, until new life takes hold and grows. This is a vital part of becoming an Edison church. Edison churches pioneer new life because they learn to fail well. As a matter of fact, failing well may be the most important thing you must learn in order to succeed.

In our pursuit of a church revival in our culture, we must give birth to pioneers. We must move people from simply being volunteers and church members into being missionaries to our own culture. We are trying to sow seeds in some very hard and rocky soil. Much of the seed we sow won't bear fruit. That doesn't necessarily mean we are doing it wrong. It just means we have to work the soil more, plant more seed in more fields, and keep doing the difficult work of cultivating. Over time, we know that seed will grow and life will emerge. We know it because the seed we are sowing is good seed. It is the best seed. We have absolute faith in that seed. We are willing to risk everything because of that seed.

The seed of the grace that has been planted within each new life in Christ always has the DNA of reproduction and pioneering. This is who we are as the church. We are a people who exist because the kingdom of God empowers everyday people to go forth and join God in bringing about new life in unexpected places. As we look at the struggles of the church around us, we should be encouraged. The key to unlocking the future of the church is within us. God has already prepared us for the challenges we face. God has pre-wired us to reproduce, to pioneer life in new places, and to overcome the obstacles in front of us. In fact, that is why we exist.

Rediscovering and embracing this part of our communal life requires courage. This is not the church we have experienced or been trained to lead. This is something new, but it is also something old. This is the original design of the church. The future of the church is not going to be written by exceptional individuals who are so uniquely gifted that they live a life none of us can hope to imitate. The future of the church is going to be written by everyday people, church leaders, and pastors who commit themselves to the hard and patient work of cultivating innovation through failure.

Now we offer ten stories of these everyday pioneers and the lessons they have learned along the way. Through their efforts and imaginative experiments, the Spirit is playing midwife as the church is being born again among us.

3

The Chinese Church That Speaks English and Spanish

Name: Trinity

Denomination: Church of the Nazarene

Location: San Gabriel Valley, California

Size: Large (300)

Ethnic Makeup: 45% Asian; 35% Latin American; 19% Caucasian; 1% African American

WHILE SUNDAY MORNINGS remain the most racially segregated hour of the week in much of the United States, Trinity Church of the Nazarene gathers as an exception. Trinity traces its heritage back ninety years, when members of Los Angeles First Church of the Nazarene started a Sunday school class for the Chinese community in 1927. Church members walked the streets of their neighborhood on Sunday mornings, inviting immigrants from China and Hong Kong to join them for class in the church basement.

Over time, this class transformed into a congregation of its own, becoming too large to continue meeting in the basement at L.A. First. In 1944, the Chinese congregation bought a house on the corner of Trinity Street and 21st Street in L.A., accompanied by a sign that said "Chinese Mission." By 1950, the church had incorporated as First Chinese Church of the Nazarene. Having outgrown the house they'd purchased, they bought land and built a church at Jefferson Avenue and Trinity Street, just blocks from their previous location.

Over the years, the demographics in their Los Angeles neighborhood changed dramatically, becoming predominantly African American and Latino. At the same time, Monterey Park, eight miles east of downtown Los Angeles, was transforming, with hundreds of Chinese-speaking immigrants moving into the area and changing the city almost overnight. First Chinese Church felt they would have a stronger future if they relocated to Monterey Park, where they could continue their ministry to the Chinese community.

Unlike many Anglo churches, who leave cities out of fear of their neighbors, First Chinese made the move to Monterey Park in order to continue their mission to Chinese people. They were able to share a church building with another Nazarene church whose numbers were declining. When that congregation decided to close its doors, First Chinese took over the building with gratitude and changed their name to Trinity Church of the Nazarene. Their new name was a tribute to their original location on Trinity Street and started them on a trajectory of welcoming people of all ethnicities.[1]

Revitalizing Trinity through Innovation

When Rev. Albert Hung became the senior pastor of Trinity in 2008, the congregation was primarily an English-speaking congregation with a Mandarin ministry. As a multi-ethnic congregation, English was the common language among different individuals and groups. Over the years, Trinity had experienced significant decline. The church lost an entire generation of people just before Albert came as a result of disagreements revolving around the inclusion of teenagers from the neighborhood in their ministry. This clash left few young adults and young families at the church. Instead of chalking up the exodus to the mistakes of someone else and leaving it at that, Albert took a humble posture. He personally pursued the members who had left, asking why they'd left and inviting them to tell their stories. He didn't attempt to persuade them to return to Trinity; he merely listened and learned. Trinity faced a challenging scenario in recovering from these past mistakes in a declining congregation. Several new endeavors in Albert's first year of leadership got the ball rolling in the right direction.

Albert and Christine (Albert's wife, who would later join the staff as a campus pastor) started a group called The Fellowship, a weekly dinner group of young adults with whom they were already acquainted. The goal of the group, from Albert and Christine's perspective, was to invest in young people as they moved through their twenties, helping them remain connected to the church during a season when many young adults leave.

Trinity also hired Sandra Wong, a longtime member, to become the director of the Christian school connected to the church. She quickly turned the struggling school around and launched a season of growth.

Albert focused on leadership development almost immediately. He and the church board read *Comeback Churches*, by Ed Stetzer and Mike Dodson, leading them to craft a new mission statement: "to make disciples of Jesus in the nations." They hoped to better reflect the diversity of their community in Monterey Park in order to become a church for all ethnicities, not only for Asian Americans. The church board also restructured the budget, which had been neglected for years. This restructuring empowered them to take some leaps of faith by hiring new staff, including a youth pastor and a Mandarin Ministries pastor.

Over the next year and a half, Trinity continued expanding their staff. In addition to hiring an administrative assistant, Trinity also brought on Pastor Johnny Cabrera, a Mexican American, as the associate pastor. A key point of innovation for Trinity is that, instead of investing in facilities by remodeling the building or heavily upgrading technology, Trinity invests in people. They believe that leaders, rather than physical space, do the work of making disciples.

With a larger staff and renewed energy, Trinity set out to meet their neighbors in diverse Monterey Park. They also needed their neighbors to meet *them* since the community didn't really know about the church. These efforts required enormous intentionality and learning, since church members didn't know where to begin. They focused on meeting neighbors through two main avenues: creating opportunities and forming partnerships. For example, they held worship services in a nearby park's amphitheater, followed by a barbecue and games. Next, at a city-sponsored carnival, the church hosted a face-painting table. They also advertised around the neighborhood, offering ESL and marriage classes at the church for residents of the local community.

However, Trinity made a big step forward by innovating a simple service project. Churches often struggle with how to serve and connect with their neighbors. Many traditional outreach events bring people into church facilities but fail to make meaningful connections with those who come. Further, such events often center on entertainment, such as a concert or Easter egg hunt, instead of serving neighbors.

A layperson had a different idea of how to serve Trinity's neighbors and make deeper connections: free oil changes for single mothers. He shared his idea with Pastor Johnny and started asking around to find out if others who had this skill were interested in joining him in offering it to the community. Unfortunately, no one else in the congregation could proficiently change the oil on a vehicle. Instead of giving up, this determined layperson kept sharing his idea with leaders of different teams, and his enthusiasm was contagious. He ended up hosting four training sessions on how to perform a proper oil change in order to prepare everyone for the service project. Concurrently, the women's group began planning activities for the mothers and children that would give the single moms something to do while waiting for their cars and also open the door for developing relationships.

All of this groundwork paid off with a successful Saturday morning service project. To make sure they were fully prepared with enough filters and oil, they scheduled and filled all of the time slots before the event. On the day of the event, when a car pulled up for its appointment, a group of eager preteens greeted them from a check-in table, registered the car for its scheduled service, and directed the family to the church's gym. Inside, a huge breakfast spread awaited the service recipients, later replaced by pizza at lunchtime. Two craft tables and a bounce house entertained the children. Adult volunteers stood by, supervising and watching them play, so their mothers could sit back and relax. The moms sat around the tables and chatted with volunteer women from Trinity. At one table, the moms could use craft materials to make homemade greeting cards if they so desired. At another, two members sat with a sign that communicated their willingness to pray with anyone who wanted that kind of support.

Trinity's innovative service event met a need for members of the community, demonstrated thoughtful hospitality to guests, and also created an important space for connections to be formed. An oil change takes at least forty-five minutes. During that time, members of Trinity took the opportunity to meet their neighbors, make connections with them, find out if their kids went to school together, or simply listen to their stories. Trinity made the space inviting and entered into such great conversations that, even when women were notified that their cars were finished, many chose to stay longer. They were given the opportunity to connect with others moms or enjoy a second cup of coffee—without having to corral their kids. Who'd want to hurry away when offered such respite?

In addition to the oil-change service event, Trinity made inroads on several partnerships as well, joining the good work already taking place in their community and filling in where there were gaps of organization and networking. Trinity became the founding member of the Monterey Park Ministerial Association, a network of pastors and churches in the city who support one another as they work toward their common goal of sharing the gospel. Trinity was the first church in their community to join the Chamber of Commerce. They participated in the Family Promise of San Gabriel Valley Network, a coalition of churches that work together to help homeless families find affordable housing. Albert also became a volunteer chaplain at the Monterey Park Police Department.

Numerous hours of training, leadership development, and formation have gone into shaping and teaching the members of Trinity Church to invest in those outside their own walls. And all of this effort and energy has not been in vain. Within just a few years, Trinity began to harvest the fruits of their labor as the sanctuary slowly filled again, as people were baptized, and as life groups gathered weekly throughout the city. By 2014, Trinity had added a second English service on Sunday mornings. Though the pastoral staff struggled to get this service off the ground initially, the change helped propel leadership to continue dreaming about what God might have in store next, now that the church had become vibrant, healthy, and in need of more space.

Trinity Merges with Hillside

As Trinity reached capacity in Monterey Park, a nearby Nazarene church struggled to stay afloat. Hillside Community Church, located in the mostly Asian American neighborhood in Rowland Heights, needed a new pastor who would be willing to lead and revitalize their waning congregation. Hillside, though small, held two worship services, one in English and one in Spanish. The district superintendent and Albert began to discuss the possibility of merging the two churches into one, multi-campus church. The leadership teams from both churches began talking about what a merger might entail. Albert, Christine, and Johnny started to preach at Hillside on a rotation, getting to know the church community while sharing about the missional and cultural DNA of Trinity. In April 2016, both churches voted overwhelmingly to approve the merger, with 98% voting in its favor.

Now Trinity functions as one church with two campuses. Albert remains the senior pastor, but each location has its own campus pastor who acts as a supervisor to other staff members at that campus. The campus pastors (Christine and Johnny) each preach primarily at the campus where they pastor, and Albert preaches at both campuses on a rotating basis.

This innovative use of resources saved Trinity from funding a building campaign to expand the Monterey Park campus through construction or the purchase of new land. At the same time, the merger resurrected Hillside Community (now called Trinity Rowland Heights) from near death. Thirty members from the Monterey Park campus, who mostly live closer to the new campus, permanently transitioned to Rowland Heights. One longtime member of Hillside Community describes the merger: "It's God's miracle to have our new brothers and sisters come help our church." With relief in her voice and tears in her eyes, she reflects on a youth-led worship service with joy. "It's been so long since we've had youth."

Merging the two congregations has presented other challenges, though. First, it was difficult to anticipate how much loss the Monterey Park campus would feel after sending thirty members to the Rowland Heights campus. Even with supportive members, those left behind at Monterey Park began to feel as if they needed to slow down some of the changes. The hardest part of the merger, in Christine's view, has been establishing the mindset of being one congregation with five different worship services (two in English, one in Mandarin, one in Spanish, and one that is culturally Filipino but uses a language mixture of predominantly English with occasional Tagalog).

A turning point in the journey toward unity occurred when youth from all five services went on a combined mission trip to Mexico. Christine describes waiting in the church parking lot with anticipation for all the youth to return home. She witnessed her first glimpse of real unity when all the parents of kids from all five services stood together talking while they eagerly awaited the safe return of their children.

It will take continued intentional effort to keep moving the two campuses toward feeling and acting as one church. By meeting weekly as a church staff, with representatives from all five services and languages, the pastors hope to build deeper relationships with one another and to ensure they are moving in the same direction. Trinity is also experimenting with joint events that would be open to members of all services. To overcome the language barriers, they are trying to practice intentional hospitality to make these joint events safe spaces for non-English speakers.

A Healthy, Multi-ethnic Congregation

In a group interview, we asked several Trinity congregants, "How do you do it? How does this work? Many churches attempt to be racially, ethnically, and culturally diverse but fail. You're doing it, and it's working." Instead of listing all of the obstacles they have overcome, most members acted nonchalant, as if it wasn't a big deal or point of great success. Their geographical location in Los Angeles is one significant reason for this attitude, of course. They already live, work, shop, and eat with and among people of different backgrounds, so it doesn't seem strange to them to worship that way too. As Albert explains, "South Monterey Park is heavily Latino and Asian American. It only makes sense that, if this is the community we're in, we would look like that."

Many congregants have spouses of different ethnic heritage from themselves, which also normalizes diversity in the church family. For Trinity to be multicultural is simply to be who they are. One couple, George and Grace, have been members of Trinity for forty-five years, since the time when it was still named First Chinese Church of the Nazarene. Grace (from a Japanese family) and George (from a Chinese family) married at a time when intermarriage between Japanese and Chinese was taboo. But Grace and George felt at home at Trinity, welcomed and loved all those years ago. They have faithfully attended and served for almost five decades.

While, in many respects, the diversity at Trinity is natural, sustaining a congregation with such diversity requires an enormous amount of effort. This intentionality begins with the hiring of a diverse staff. Albert is Chinese American, a second-generation immigrant from Canada. Christine is Korean Canadian. Albert previously served as the international chaplain at Azusa Pacific University, giving him extensive experience working with international people. Both he and Christine understand from their own experiences what it is like to be foreigners or immigrants. Johnny, the campus pastor at Monterey Park, is Mexican American. He explains, "I can be another face of Trinity for people to connect with." In addition to the supervising campus pastors (Johnny and Christine), each campus also has specific pastors who oversee the non-English services, so Monterey Park and Rowland Heights each have their own Mandarin pastor, and Rowland Heights also has separate pastors for the Spanish and Filipino services. By consistently meeting together as a staff, they are continually connecting to maintain their identity and values as one church.

For Trinity to reach the people around them, they have to think differently than a church that is, for the most part, ethnically homogenous. Trinity's mindset includes an openness toward and awareness of other cultures, as opposed to unconsciously catering only to one culture. This attitude requires thoughtful consideration of others and flexibility and humility when cultural differences collide.

A spirit of curiosity is another central component of the mindset at Trinity, and Albert and the staff work hard to foster this spirit in the congregation. As Albert explains, "You can't be colorblind and make this work." Curiosity encourages the desire to learn about another person's perspective, culture, and experience, instead of shutting it down or refusing to engage.

The pastors purposefully cultivate cultural skill development through sermons, classes, discipleship mentoring, and community events. For example, one skill required to faithfully be the church rooted in a community is knowing your neighbors. Trinity teaches people how to go out to their neighborhoods as amateur ethnographers and ask, "Who lives in this area? What ethnicities are they? What languages do they speak?"

Furthermore, Trinity created a repeating, six-week series called "Love Where You Live" that encourages Trinity's community groups to intentionally connect with the neighborhoods where they live. Groups have attended city council meetings, hosted block parties, brought dinners to the police station, provided breakfast for teachers of a local school, and invited city officials to come share at their worship services about issues like homelessness. The end of the six-week series culminates in an open house on both church campuses, where members invite all the people they encountered and interacted with over the last six weeks to visit Trinity.

Learning the differences in leadership style across cultures is another important skill required of Trinity staff. Western and Asian cultures differ significantly in their approach to leadership, confrontation, and management. Negotiating these divergent approaches is essential in much of the work of the church, from leading the church board to offering pastoral care. Everyone at Trinity navigates the nuances of culture in order to be in relationship with one another. Awkward interactions or unintentional offenses inevitably occur. The dynamics of age, gender, and positions of leadership vary greatly at Trinity. Nurturing a flexible and generous attitude, one that is willing both to correct and be corrected, helps everyone learn from their mistakes and continue to live as faithful witnesses to God's diverse kingdom.

Innovation: Let Go of the Curriculum

Every Sunday morning, a group of eight to twelve women of different ages and ethnicities gather in Christine's Sunday school class. She sensed that the women had major trepidation about how to read and study Scripture—whether on their own or together. For years, they had relied on a set curriculum to guide their class discussions. One Sunday morning, Christine proposed that they begin a new study—this time, with the Bible and nothing else. The room filled with an awkward silence, but they eventually agreed to give it a try.

Next, Christine passed out printed-off, double-spaced copies of the book of Ephesians and conducted some initial training on inductive Bible study methods. She encouraged the group members to ask God to speak through the Word as they studied it during the week and then brought their questions or insights to class the following Sunday.

"During our group sessions," Christine reflects, "the Bible sprang to life as the women began to share their discoveries. It was like having a grand spiritual potluck, where we each brought to the table all the golden nuggets the Lord laid in our laps during the week. I can't fully describe to you the swell of joy in my heart as I watched these women feed each other with love and encouragement. No one left hungry. Everyone left feeling blessed and satisfied."[2] Today, Christine's innovative Bible study class is co-ed and available on both campuses.

Embracing Innovation and the Failure It Requires

Over the last nine years, Trinity has transformed from a struggling and aging congregation to a thriving and diverse congregation. Most of Trinity's innovation relates to their transition from being inwardly focused in mindset and practice to being outwardly focused through serving their community and making disciples.

Albert sees the role of innovator as a key part of his leadership. He believes that you have to try things to find out what works and doesn't work because you don't know until you try. Through all his experiences at Trinity, he cautions that innovation must be handled with care. Leaders often underestimate the cost of change. "Every time we ask people to change," Albert points out, "we are using up our leadership capital." It's challenging to balance innovation and resistance. Often, older members feel alienated amidst innovation, as if the church is slipping away from them. The leader then has to decide whether to keep going forward or to pause. In some cases, this means tracking people down to ensure they know they are not forgotten and that their presence matters to the community, even as things change. Calibrating change and managing stress in the congregation require much more energy than most leaders expect.

Throughout the innovation process, Albert considers communication to be key. The leader cannot assume that the congregation knows what changes are happening and why; leaders must explain everything. Albert handles communication by cultivating transparency in the innovation process. He openly explains that what is about to happen will be tough, but he also casts a vision of hope for what could be. He spends a lot of energy framing each big step, communicating with the congregation on at least four points: 1) Why the change is occurring; 2) What the time frame is; 3) What the change will cost (finances, resources, and relationships); 4) Some kind of buffer to account for what the church or leader doesn't yet know.

That last point is critical. Albert explains, "We simply can't afford to wait around forever, trying to perfect our plans. It's better to get to 80-percent readiness and then start, just to get things moving, and make adjustments as we go. By admitting that failure is a real possibility—but not an excuse for inaction—we create a buffer for all the hiccups and mistakes we'll make along the way. Sometimes the buffer takes the form of overestimating the time frame, manpower, or finances needed for a particular initiative. Sometimes it's just a matter of letting people know we don't have it all figured out and that that's okay."

For Albert, failure is an inevitable part of innovation. Some churches are afraid to name failures because leaders are emotionally invested in their efforts. However, Trinity has openly experimented with plenty of innovations—many that worked and some that did not. They planned outreach events that flopped. They alarmed people with their experiments in conversational preaching; although they gave it a try, they found great resistance in their context. They planned some Friday night programming that didn't work because it required a large time commitment from the leaders but garnered little investment from those who came. On the other hand, many other innovations *did* work. Slowly, the church realized that risking trial and error is the only way to know if something *will* work.

Their willingness to embrace innovation and the failure it requires was essential in bringing Trinity to where they are today. As the newness of the merger wears off and they figure out what's working and what isn't, more flexibility, communication, and innovation will be needed to make the transition work. For those at Trinity, innovation is not primarily about being cutting-edge, staying current with cultural trends, or even maintaining their multicultural community. Trinity innovates simply to be faithful in making disciples and loving their neighbors.

Learn More

- https://onetrinitychurch.org/
- Christine Hung, "Just the Bible: When We Study God's Word Together No One Leaves Hungry," *The Table*, http://www.thetablemagazine.org/articles/18-stories/28-just-the-bible-when-we-study-god-s-word-together-no-one-leaves-hungry.
- Albert Hung, "Feeding Each Other: Get the Most Out of Your Group Bible Study by Following These Five Key Principles," *The Table,* http://www.thetablemagazine.org/articles/18-stories/29-feeding-each-other-get-the-most-out-of-your-group-bible-study-by-following-these-five-key-principles
- "A Love Story for Us All (Monterey Park)," *The Table,* http://www.thetablemagazine.org/categories/23-bible-church-profile/46-a-love-story-for-us-all-monterey-park

Recommended Resources

- *Pursuing God's Will Together: A Discernment Practice for Leadership Groups,* by Ruth Haley Barton (2012)
- *Better Together: Making Church Mergers Work,* by Jim Tomberlin and Warren Bird (2012)
- *Comeback Churches: How 300 Churches Turned Around and Yours Can Too,* by Ed Stetzer and Mike Dodson (2007)

Discussion Questions

1. How does the history of your local church shape who you are today?

2. Does your congregation reflect the races, ethnicities, and cultures of the people who live in the neighborhood surrounding the church building? If not, why?

3. How does your congregation meet people who are not part of your church? How could your church be intentional about making connections?

4. Is your church nervous about innovation or change? If so, what is the source of this fear, and how might you begin to overcome it?

5. Is your church able to name failures without fear? What are some instances of failure after trying something new or different? How have you handled it?

6. How does your church engage in serving your community? Do these practices provide meaningful opportunities for lasting, relational connections with people?

4

The Church That Became a Refuge for Refugees

Church Name: Westbury

Denomination: United Methodist Church

Location: Houston, Texas

Size: Medium (200)

Ethnic Makeup: 55% Caucasian; 37% African American; 4% Asian; 3% Hispanic; 1% Multiethnic

"WHO IS MY NEIGHBOR? Where is God already at work?" Westbury United Methodist Church began asking these questions in 2010 as they came to terms with the state of their church and mission. When they constructed their church building in 1965, Westbury was situated in an upper-middle-class suburb of Houston. However, following the 1980s oil bust, the neighborhood became increasingly lower income. Today, the Westbury area is home to refugees from all over the globe—particularly

El Salvador, Eritrea, Burundi, Bhutan, Democratic Republic of Congo, and Rwanda.[1]

The congregation at Westbury UMC has a long history of multicultural diversity. In the 1970s, Westbury's first two African American families joined the predominantly white congregation, and Westbury has been racially diverse ever since. The willingness of these two families to invest deeply, despite the risks, helped embed multiculturalism in the DNA of the church. In 2010, when the congregation began their missional rediscovery, their members already included Anglos, African Americans, and African immigrants.[2] Still, the members at Westbury reflected a mere snapshot of the diversity of their surrounding neighborhoods, and the church was largely homogeneous economically.

In 2010, the bishop appointed Pastor Tommy Williams to Westbury, hoping that Tommy would breathe new life into this declining congregation with great potential. Over time, Westbury had become too inward focused, losing its evangelistic impulse and missional clarity.[3] The church needed leadership who could help them discern how to be the church *here*, in this particular time and place. Since Tommy had attended Westbury as a teenager, he had the trust of the congregation right away, even as he began to make changes.

Tommy quickly led the congregation into a process of discernment, encouraging people to take inventory of their gifts and to dream about how they could use them in ministry. Through preaching on mission and discipleship, meeting in small discussion groups in homes, and creating a discernment work group, Westbury drafted new vision and mission statements and redefined their core values.[4] Their mission, vision, and identity centered on one focal point: "Westbury is a church for all people—people of all ages, races, and nations." While the church was already racially and culturally diverse to a degree, Tommy felt that diversity was not shaping their life together in worship, mission, or discipleship.[5] Westbury renewed their commitment to multicultural inclusivity as the central component of their mission.

The first concrete change occurred in Sunday worship. Westbury hired DeAndre Johnson to be the associate pastor for music and worship. DeAndre has a passion for multicultural music and immediately began to integrate an eclectic mix of music into weekly Sunday worship. The church leadership then invited social activists John Perkins and Shane Claiborne to come for a panel conversation during morning worship service on World Communion Sunday in 2011. This discussion began some congregational education on paradigms of ministry, including Christian community development and intentional Christian community. They began to dream about what it might look like for Westbury to take these kinds of approaches to ministering outside their walls and connecting with their neighbors.

While the leadership at Westbury circled around these questions, Tommy got a call from a stranger—an apartment manager at a nearby complex near Fondren Road, just three miles from the church. The manager asked Tommy to "send somebody down sometime to start a Bible study." Almost as soon as Westbury leaders asked where God was already at work, a neighbor of theirs literally invited the church to spend time *with their neighbors*. Meanwhile, Nusura Mtendamema had been attending Westbury for about a year and a half. Nusura, a refugee from Burundi, heard about Westbury from a friend and began attending regularly, even though she spoke little English. Nusura lived in one of the apartment complexes on Fondren Road.

The pastors and lay leadership interpreted these connections as an invitation from God to pursue something further with their neighbors who reside in the apartment complexes in the Fondren area. They also discerned that the ministry to which God was calling them was not a short-term one. Instead, they cast a vision for an incarnational residential ministry.

Hiring a Pastor to Listen

Westbury decided to bring a pastor on staff to do the slow work of listening to their neighbors and leading Westbury into the places where God was already at work. This new community pastor would live and work in the Fondren community. They didn't have the money to bring on another full-time pastor midway through the budget year, but that didn't stop them. As a result of reaching out with their vision in hand, Westbury received denominational support and donations from individuals, enabling them to move forward with their dream.[6]

Tommy and the church board called Hannah Terry, fresh out of seminary, to relocate to Houston and begin this work. Hannah felt clearly called by God to "listening to others through the Holy Spirit" and working with people toward answers that don't come quickly.[7] Hannah had training in intentional Christian community and Christian community development through her internship at New Song Community Church in

Baltimore. This veteran Christian community development (CCD)[8] congregation birthed a ministry and a church after three Christians intentionally moved into the Sandtown neighborhood in Baltimore to follow Jesus and to be good neighbors.[9] At New Song, Hannah discovered her calling: to move into a neighborhood and to make friends, which was exactly what Westbury wanted.

Hannah articulates the starting place for her work with this new, unknown, and undefined ministry as follows:

1) to be faithful disciples of Jesus who welcome the presence and power of the Holy Spirit;

2) to engage the new ministry as an entire body with the neighborhood in the Fondren corridor;

3) to deepen relationships with God and one another by living, eating, working, and communing together in home spaces;

4) to listen intently and faithfully to the Holy Spirit and the voices within the community;

5) to slow down and notice the details; to be attentive to God's work in the world and how Westbury United Methodist Church is welcomed into being God's partners in it.[10]

Hannah began her first week of ministry at Fondren by visiting Nusura, the Burundian refugee who had been attending Westbury. Tommy asked Hannah to discern how God was at work in Nusura. All Hannah knew before making the visit was that Nusura was a refugee from Burundi, spoke no English, and lived at Los Arcos Apartments off Fondren. Hannah describes her first visit to Nusura's home, during which Hannah greeted Nusura with a plate of brownies in hand:

I approached Nusura Mtendamema with a smile. I tried not to act like a totally-amped-and-naive-for Jesus, brand-new seminary grad—but that's what I was. When we met at her apartment, we sat on her couch. We looked into each other's eyes. We giggled nervously. We said a few phrases in our respective languages, but we mainly laughed and embraced the friendly silence.

Slowly, the sacred, gracious and powerful presence of God in Nusura's home overwhelmed me. We had both shown up—each with our own particular clothing, culture, language, expectations, personality and story. And we found ourselves present to God between us.[11]

This first visit to Nusura's home, awkward and holy, became a crucial step of innovation for the Fondren Apartment Ministry (FAM). FAM is fundamentally about showing up and listening. This approach differs from the ways many churches engage in ministry outside church walls because it is not a top-down approach, where church leadership make the decision on how they will help. It is also not a church bus approach, where the church goes to neighborhoods far away, fills the bus with people, brings them to church, and then takes them back. The goal of FAM is not to recruit new members to swell Westbury's attendance rolls. Hannah explains, "FAM involves living in solidarity and working with people in the neighborhood surrounding our church in Houston."[12] FAM isn't even a refugee ministry, although refugees happen to be the primary demographic to whom they minister. Their work with refugees grew out of simply showing up, listening, and finding out how God was already working.

Hannah spent the next several months learning everything she could about the Fondren neighborhood. She spent hours walking and driving around, meeting and listening to as many community members as possible—Fondren residents, social workers, police officers, shop owners, and community leaders.[13] "I needed to understand this neighborhood and Houston and Westbury," Hannah explains, "and I wanted to learn from any source that I could learn from. It was like a big puzzle that I was trying to figure out."[14]

In October 2012, Westbury participated in National Night Out at two complexes in Fondren: Los Arcos, the 516-unit complex where Nusura lived, and the complex that had originally extended the invitation to Westbury to hold a Bible study. Members of Westbury came to meet residents of the apartments and enjoy food together. They hoped it would be clear after these two events where it was that God was leading them to focus their energy and attention. The Spirit made it totally clear: Los Arcos was the place. With Nusura already living at Los Arcos, she helped to establish trust between the refugee community and the folks from Westbury. She was the link they needed to begin this work.

Westbury brought Hannah on board with the hope that she and others would move into the Fondren area and practice intentional Christian community. Together with three others, Hannah moved into the neighborhood in March 2013. Daniel and Lindsey, a couple from Westbury, sensed God's urging to join this ministry, and they also moved into the complex. Eric, an asylum seeker himself, made the move from Dallas to Houston to minister with FAM after being introduced to Hannah through a mutual friend. Because Los Arcos had the most affordable housing in the area, these four did not feel comfortable taking apart-

An Innovator's Identity Challenge

Hannah uprooted her whole world to come to Houston and start FAM. She moved across the country, leaving behind friends, family, and familiarity to do this work. Starting something from scratch can easily become all-consuming, especially for the leader. After pouring herself into this work constantly for several years, she faced a hard realization.

Hannah explains it like this: "Three years in, my identity was completely tied up in the success or failure of FAM. I was scared about whether it would live or die. I didn't have a healthy practice of Sabbath. The message of God's grace and boundless love—what FAM is all about—I didn't believe it for myself. God revealed to me, gently and graciously, that even as the pastor of FAM, God likes and loves me. I too am beloved. Because of that, because I'm loved, I can release the results of this experiment. It's free. I'm not responsible."

Many pastors and innovators face a similar struggle, but God can heal that self-proving drive in all of us. Hannah suggests that innovators should pay attention to our hunger for affirmation or tying our worth to results. We need to ask God to change that in us so that we receive affirmation from God and find freedom in releasing back to God what is already God's.

ments from refugee families who needed the least expensive option. Instead, they moved into the Reserve at Bankside, an apartment complex just one mile north of Los Arcos on Fondren Road. This move marked the beginning of ten months of practicing intentional Christian community, a practice that included daily morning prayer, weekly dinners, and hosting potlucks for their new neighbors.[15]

The Potluck Explodes

In April of 2013, the intentional community members invited several friends from Los Arcos to Daniel and Lindsey's apartment for a potluck dinner. They hoped this would become a simple weekly meal together with a few neighbors. Fifteen people showed up for dinner that first time. The third week, thirty people attempted to squeeze into their apartment.

They had never expected such exponential growth, but it quickly became clear that meeting in an individual apartment was not a sustainable option. Thankfully, Houston's warm weather makes meeting outdoors possible throughout most of the year. The next Wednesday night, they cooked hot dogs outside at Los Arcos, and more than eighty people—mostly children—showed up for what eventually became weekly Wednesday Community Nights. Hannah had no idea so many people would be interested in participating. In the back of their minds, they allowed themselves to imagine that maybe, someday a long time down the road, FAM might turn into house churches or small Bible study groups meeting in homes, but they were prepared to build slowly. They were blown away that the number of people interested in Wednesday Community Nights was so high from the beginning.

For five straight months, they held Wednesday Community Nights, which consisted of the same loose pattern from week to week. The group began by circling up to sing together and pray the Lord's Prayer in a repeat-after-me format. Then they provided food, games, arts and crafts, sidewalk chalk, and bubbles. Sometimes a volunteer would led a Bible lesson. Always, there was abundant conversation. During the summer, Hannah and her team helped arrange for the Los Arcos kids to participate in a few enrichment programs. First, they participated in a fine arts camp at Westbury Baptist Church. Then the kids joined Freedom School, a literacy program that is geared toward racial justice and held at Westbury UMC.

We Want to Come to Your Church

One August evening, following Wednesday Community Night, several kids, teenagers, and adults swarmed Hannah with one clear message: "Pastor, we want to come to your church!" Hannah couldn't believe what they were asking. She had been clear all along that FAM's purpose was not to save a struggling congregation by getting more bodies in the door of the church. Hannah admits that, while most pastors would rejoice at the request to attend Westbury, she felt disappointed. She and her team were planning to experiment to see how FAM might push the envelope on traditional forms of church.[16]

The more Hannah talked with leaders in the refugee community, the more she understood why refugees wanted to become a part of Westbury. After being forcefully uprooted from their homes and enduring the hardships endemic to refugees, the established church appealed to them. Unlike many young adults in the United States who are disillusioned with institutions, the refugee community desired the safety and stability of a traditional church. Within a few weeks of making it clear to Hannah what they wanted, refugees from the apartments began to attend church at Westbury. Hannah arranged Sunday morning transportation to and from the church so that need wouldn't keep people away.

What about the Liability?

Insurance liability issues can stifle innovation in churches; it's downright embarrassing to admit. How many pastors have shared a dream in a church board meeting, only to hear the response, "What about the liability?"

At Westbury, the liability question came up when Hannah requested help from members to transport folks from Los Arcos to church on Sundays. Hannah and other leaders simply reframed the request in such a way that that the liability question lost its relevance; church members were merely picking up their friends and driving them to church. "If you invited one of your friends to church," they reasoned, "you wouldn't be concerned about them riding in your car because of liability. It wouldn't even cross your mind. This is no different. These are our friends. It's not a church bus that carts people to church. It's friends picking up friends. Driving friends to church is a simple act of discipleship. It's a way that we are taking a risk together on behalf of what God is doing in our neighborhood."

We Want You to Start an English School

In September, another direct request came from the community: "Pastor, please start an English school." Hannah and her team could have set their own agenda for what the community needed. The needs were certainly abundant: language, space for community meetings, employment, transportation, and more. But Hannah knew that the trust and relationship building had to happen first so that the community members themselves could decide what was most important to them. The people were setting their own agenda for addressing their own needs.

While there were other opportunities for refugees to learn English, scheduling conflicts and limited transportation made it nearly impossible for most Fondren residents to take advantage of ESL classes elsewhere. Furthermore, since many refugees come from tribal cultures that don't traditionally teach reading and writing, some needed curriculum geared toward someone who is preliterate.

Holly Wetly, a member of Westbury, began to teach English classes twice a week at Los Arcos so that residents wouldn't have to travel to study. She had twelve students complete her course in the first year. Since then, FAM has partnered with other organizations, such as Literacy Advocate and International Emergency Development Aid and Relief, both to develop curriculum and to offer additional ESL classes.[17]

This pattern of listening to the community remained FAM's most important innovation in the years that followed. Hannah and others continued to do the slow work of making friendships, building trust, listening to the community, and responding to the needs and hopes the community brought forth. Many of the additional resources and partnerships FAM has now (job training, transportation, and growing food—both to eat and to sell) originated in simply listening to the community.

As FAM has transitioned into a more structured ministry—including developing a board of directors—the emphasis on listening has remained at the forefront. FAM desires their leadership to reflect a redistribution of power so that the board includes 50 percent Fondren residents or refugees and 50 percent Westbury or FAM team members. This commitment has not been easy. Language is often a barrier. The time required to serve on a board is expensive for refugees, who often work many hours each week to provide for their families. Differing cultural dynamics raise additional challenges. Still, though, this slow and collaborative decision-making process enables a diverse group of people to respond to the needs of the community after having listened first.

Westbury Today: A Church Transformed

Westbury United Methodist Church continues to ask, "Who is my neighbor? Where is God already at work?" After six years of asking these questions with openness to the Holy Spirit, it is obvious how God has transformed this church. Westbury lives into their mission to be a church for all people in new and important ways because of the Fondren Apartment Ministry. FAM started a trajectory at Westbury of listening to neighbors, listening to the Spirit, and being willing to adapt. For example, Westbury developed a beautiful synergy of meeting their needs and the needs of their refugees by utilizing their resources to create a commercial cleaning internship. The internship meets Westbury's need to fill this important staff position while also providing a refugee with one full year of stable employment, job training, and English classes paid for by FAM.

Westbury has become a church that rallies around social impact and hope. Westbury's deep concern for their neighbors and for God's justice reminds Hannah of a quote attributed to St. Augustine: "Hope has two beautiful daughters; their names are Anger and Courage. Anger at the way things are, and Courage to see that they do not remain as they are." This anger and courage, rooted in God's hope, drive much of how Westbury engages in their own congregational life and in missional partnerships.

Following the massacre at Emanuel AME Church in Charleston, South Carolina, in 2015, Westbury facilitated difficult conversations in the congregation by confronting the wounds of racism with the hope of healing. Together they mourned the sins of prejudice and the loss of these brothers and sisters in Christ. Lay leaders at Westbury "committed to long-haul justice work through the healing of racism."[18] In July 2015, Westbury leaders began to meet together for dinner to share stories of their personal experiences of race. Facilitators from the nearby Center for the Healing of Racism[19] assisted in these conversations. They hoped to become better equipped to respond to racism in Houston and even in their own congregation.

For many members of Westbury, despite the church's multicultural history, the aftermath of the Charleston church shooting was the first time they had talked openly about racism and the way it keeps them from deeper relationships. Hannah explains, "The groups are exploring the ways the church has much to do within its own walls to say yes to freedom, yes to reconciliation, and yes to the gospel of Jesus Christ so that the church can be a community of healing beyond walls with the city and the world."[20]

These conversations among lay leaders led to a six-week community reading of Dr. Martin Luther King's "Letter from Birmingham Jail." The current senior pastor, Danny Yang, urged every member of Westbury to attend. He drew strong connections between the letters of the apostle Paul written from a jail cell and Dr. King's letter written under similar circumstances. Groups from inside and outside the church sat at round tables, read through the letter together, and participated in discussion.[21]

Today, Westbury reflects increased diversity, not only racially and culturally but also socioeconomically. Twenty-five to thirty African refugees from Fondren now worship at Westbury. While one of Westbury's key values remains "multicultural inclusivity," they still struggle to work out the differences between *diversity* and *multicultural inclusivity*. Being a diverse congregation is one important step, but embracing multicultural inclusivity is another, more challenging venture. Reflecting on the challenges of diversity, Hannah shares, "The boundaries of race, the boundaries of ethnicity, of class, of socio-economics—FAM doesn't say, 'No, these don't exist.' FAM says, 'Okay, in the midst of the boundaries, how is Christ known? How is Christ making us one?'"[22]

Other church leaders who hope to innovate in their own contexts often ask Hannah, "Can any church do this?"

Her answer is, "Absolutely. Will the results be the same? No." It won't be the same because the heart of FAM's ministry is living in solidarity and working with people in the neighborhood surrounding Westbury UMC in Houston. "What you find in your community is likely to be quite different," Hannah says. "The details of your ministry will depend on what you find."[23]

Hannah cautions that this work isn't easy. There's no innovators' user manual or blueprint showing exactly what to do; much of the work involves taking risks and being scared and uncertain.[24] However, based on her experience at FAM and additional training through the Academy for Missional Wisdom[25] with Elaine Heath, Hannah suggests these four postures for innovative listeners: show up, pay attention, join God, and release the results.[26]

The transformation and reconciliation that God has done at Westbury were shining brightly on Easter Sunday 2015. The confirmation class of ten students stepped forward to publicly affirm their faith in Christ and to join Westbury as official members. Four of the ten students came to Westbury through FAM. In the weeks leading up to Easter, the youth director was tasked with teaching a multicultural, multilingual confirmation class. Two of the boys are members of rival African tribes, having experienced deep suffering as a result of the conflict between the Hutus and Tutsis.[27] But that Easter Sunday, they stood side by side, once enemies from a horrific war and now members together in Christ's one body.

Learn More

- http://www.westburyumc.org/
- Watch a video produced by The Work of the People: http://www .theworkofthepeople.com/missional-imagination
- Watch a video produced by Houston filmmaker Marlon F. Hall and Faith and Leadership: https://www.faithandleadership.com/deep -listening-fondren-apartment-ministry

Recommended Resources

- *When Helping Hurts: How to Alleviate Poverty without Hurting the Poor . . . and Yourself*, by Steve Corbett and Briant Fikkert (2009)
- *A Mile in my Shoes: Cultivating Compassion*, by Trevor Hudson (2005)
- *Toxic Charity: How Churches and Charities Hurt Those They Help (and How to Reverse It)*, by Robert D. Lupton (2011)

Discussion Questions

1. How would your church answer Westbury's questions: Who is my neighbor? Where is God already at work?

2. Do any of your church's ministries outside your walls follow this incarnational approach, beginning with listening to the community?

3. Do any parts of the worshiping life of your church reflect multicultural inclusivity?

4. In Westbury and FAM's story, so much time was spent showing up and paying attention. Opportunities and direction for what they should be doing came from the community itself, from the initial request for a Bible study to the specific requests for help with English and employment. How could your church be paying attention and showing up where you currently aren't? What keeps you from paying attention and showing up?

5. Has your congregation engaged any critical reflection or learning on working with disenfranchised neighbors, such as reading a book (like *When Helping Hurts*) or attending a CCDA workshop? If not, what might be a good first step for you?

5

The Church of Accidental Abolitionists

Church Name: Duneland Community

Denomination: Church of the Nazarene

Location: Chesterton, Indiana

Size: Medium (115)

Ethnic Makeup: 92% Caucasian; 8% Other (Latino, Chinese, African American, Multiethnic)

EVERY STORY in the kingdom of God is essentially a story of the cross. It is a story of death bringing forth life. It is a seed being buried in the ground and new life bursting forth. It is a birth story, the birth of a child of God. This is as true for churches as it is for individuals. Every community of believers is a community filled with birth stories. A dream, a promise, a hope of a new family is planted into the soil of a community, and new life bursts forth.

For the people of Duneland Community Church, their birth story has been anything but smooth. It is filled with death, sacrifice, and the painful process of being reborn into the movement of the kingdom of God. Birthed in 1946, Chesterton Church of the Nazarene was never a church with big dreams. Chesterton, Indiana, isn't a destination for those with big dreams. Like a plant whose roots are trapped inside its tiny pot, most people who grow up in Chesterton need to move on to bigger places to begin seeking their dreams. You don't live in Chesterton to be part of the newest fad or latest craze. You live in Chesterton because you want to hold onto life as you have known it. This small, Midwestern town has been intentionally preserved by those who call it home. It is a stopover on the way to somewhere else. Most people only know of its existence because they have seen its exit sign from one of the three major highways that crisscross Chesterton. But, except for those who have stopped to visit its strip of highway-induced, fast-food restaurants, dropped by in the summer for the surprisingly robust European farmers' market, or camped at the Dunes State Park along Lake Michigan, Chesterton might as well not exist for outsiders.

In 1957, during a season of growth for the town, Chesterton Church of the Nazarene's congregation built a small church building, nestled among the alternating one-way streets of Chesterton's central residential district. The nice neighborhoods, proximity to industry-leading steel mills, and quick access to Lake Michigan made Chesterton a great place to settle down and raise a family. These values, which dominated mid-twentieth-century American Christianity, were woven into the birth of the local Nazarene church. Located in a white-clapboard building two blocks north of the high school, this small-town church was the home of good, God-fearing Midwesterners. Never very large, the steady, unpretentious congregation was a mirror image of its community.

But then something funny happened. This small church, largely unnoticed, even by its own unremarkable town, began to dream together a dream that was born, frankly, out of desperation. This was not a church with a long history of success. In its first fifty years of existence, the church had rotated through eighteen different pastors. One wonders whether the revolving staff door led the church to struggle or whether the struggles of the church led to the revolving staff door. Regardless, this was a church whose reputation preceded it, and the reputation was that they couldn't get their act together.

Let's Try Something New

While the worship and church growth methodologies of late twentieth-century evangelicalism helped many traditional churches change and grow, Chesterton Church of the Nazarene stayed true to its nature. Other churches embraced the changing world around them and invested in new worship styles, youth ministries, and outreach techniques. Chesterton was happy to continue being who they had always been. Well, *happy* may be too strong a word. They were comfortable being who they were and hoped that simply continuing on would one day, unexpectedly, lead them to break-through.

By the mid-1990s, however, it was clear that something had to change. As youth left the church and their already humble size dwindled, a growing sense of desperation began to build in the church. They were ready to try something different. Their desire to achieve breakthrough began to outweigh their comfort-induced stasis. So with the help of district leadership and a new pastor, the church began to undergo the process of re-birth. At that time, Dr. Lee Woolery led the Northwest Indiana district of the Church of the Nazarene. Lee had numerous churches like Chesterton spread through his corner of the Midwest. He faced multiple situations of desperation, where the dying remnants of traditional churches were trying to discover a way into a new future for the next generation. The district began to work with Ken Priddy—a consultant who specialized in rebirth-ing dying congregations—to help these churches reimagine their futures.

The new pastor, Shane Stillman, arrived fresh out of seminary. The Stillman family viewed Chesterton as a stopover while they prepared for Shane to serve as a military chaplain. He arrived with a clear sense of purpose to help the Chesterton church think differently. Under two and a half years of Shane's leadership, the church developed a vision, values, and an imagination. The first step, as they discovered their true purpose as a church, was to move out of their box. For Chesterton Church of the Nazarene, their building was a tiny pot suppressing their dreams. It was a safe place, hidden away from the community and allowing them to subsist without changing. It was comfortable for them, but it wasn't an inviting place to visitors or to dreamers. The confining nature of the space epitomized the church, its philosophy, and its vision. So the first sacrifice in pursuit of a new future was their home. Their building was a place to convalesce; it wasn't a place for resurrection.

Over the next year, almost everything about the church changed. As we know, resurrection can only follow death. Chesterton Church of the Nazarene had to die in order to live. If you want to test the faith of a group of Christians, ask them to sell their church building, change the name of their church, and start worshiping in a school building. If you are really a glutton for punishment, go even further and ask them to change their style of worship, hire a new pastor, and invite the whole community to join you. That is exactly what this little, unremarkable, faithful church did. They stepped out in faith and allowed who they were to die in order to step into the dream of rebirth. And the results were astonishing. Chesterton Church of the Nazarene—a sleepy and unimaginative church in an unremarkable place—was born again as Duneland Community Church. Aside from a handful of faithful members, very little about this new church resembled the old one. A new pastor, who was known for being an outside-the-box thinker, came in to lead this rebirth process. His new vision and great energy helped lead Duneland into its new life.

Ten minutes before their first public service as Duneland Community Church, there were only a handful of people gathered at the elementary school for worship. But then something remarkable happened. Reminiscent of the climactic scene in *Field of Dreams*, a line of cars suddenly appeared, and people began to stream into the school. More than two hundred people showed up that first Sunday, and new life was birthed in Chesterton.

The next several years were a grand adventure. Everything was new. Excitement and joy naturally accompanied so much movement. Stasis was left by the wayside as the Spirit began to change not just a group of people but an entire town. Many took notice as a church that had long been hidden moved out into the open and engaged in mission throughout the community. The risk of changing everything paid off in huge ways. Then the bill showed up. The markers were called in, and the gamble seemed lost.

Three years into its life as Duneland Community Church—after all that sacrifice and hard work and initial signs of promise—the entire rebirth process seemed for naught. One awful Sunday, the same district superintendent who had helped the church imagine a new future, who'd been there celebrating the huge launch, and who had pointed to Duneland as an example of what other dying churches could hope to be had to tell this growing young congregation that its innovative pastor had been asked to resign.

This abrupt change was devastating to the church. The inherent risk in trying to give birth to something new is that new life is so fragile in its early stages. This new church was filled with brand-new Christians, lifelong Christians whose faith had been radically changed, and many who were interestedly seeking out faith. There wasn't enough spiritual maturity to handle something so devastating. The roots of community and discipleship weren't yet deep enough to hold the church together during this storm. Disbelief and fear overwhelmed the faithful core who had led the rebirth and were helping this new community grow. Not many believed that their new dream would survive. And for a long time, their beliefs were justified. The next six years were hard. There was a splintering of the community. Many who were disillusioned left and started their own church. There was a reunification, of sorts, when that new church failed years later.

Learning to Dream Again

Fast-forward to 2008. Duneland had almost gone fully through its life cycle from rebirth all the way back to death. There were more people in the congregation than there had been before the rebirth, but they felt just as lost. They worshiped each week at Chesterton Middle School, about two blocks from their old building. For all their effort and sacrifice, it didn't feel like the church had gone very far. Something very important, however, had been woven into the DNA of Duneland Community Church. The process of death and resurrection altered the church significantly. There was strength—the heard-earned fruit of perseverance—hidden underneath the pain and frustration. This strength, tested and tried, sustained the church through a drought that would have killed off many other faith communities.

In the fall of 2008, Greg Arthur arrived in Chesterton to pastor Duneland Community Church. Like most local transplants, Chesterton had never been part of Greg's plan for his life or ministry. That was just fine, though—because a pastor like Greg had never been part of Duneland's dreams either. Greg was an unusual choice for them. In many ways, his calling to Duneland resulted from a willingness by the congregation to try anything. The desperation that had once encouraged them toward new dreams now encouraged them to take another risk. Before coming to Chesterton, Greg had served as the associate pastor of a Methodist church in Chapel Hill, North Carolina. At the age of thirty-one, he was not only young, but he had no experience as a senior pastor, didn't know the local culture, and had no experience revitalizing a failing church. On paper, it seemed like a mismatch. On the other hand, maybe all those things were actually what made Greg a great fit. From the beginning, he made it clear to the church that he wasn't arriving with answers. He wasn't going to come down from the mountaintop and deliver a vision for success. His job was to lead the church through a process in which they would discover God's will for them—together. So that is what they did.

About a year after Greg arrived at Duneland, they made one of their riskiest decisions. They moved out of the middle school, where they had worshiped together for the previous six years, and rented an empty warehouse at a struggling lumberyard. All of their energy, each week, had been going into making Sunday morning happen at the middle school. If they wanted to spend their energy on something else, they had to make Sunday morning easier. So they moved over to the unlikely lumberyard, where another transformation took place. An old showroom became a worship space, a glass-cutting room became a nursery, and a garage became a children's classroom. The time they spent renovating this old warehouse—days that became weeks that became months that became years—proved a unifying force for Duneland Community. Sweat equity, financial sacrifices, and the flexibility to navigate an ever-changing space bonded them as a family.

With energy to spend on something other than the Sunday service, the church focused on reconciliation and healing so that they could move past their communal trauma. Engaging in a new visioning process, everyone in the church was invited into a dialogue about who God was calling Duneland to be. They open-sourced the process, inviting feedback, regularly updating the congregation about the conversations they were having, and sharing every decision in as close to real time as they could.

What emerged from these years were the foundational planks upon which the future of the church would be rebuilt. First, the church members started to like each other again. It is amazing how much more fun it is to be the church when you actually like the people in your church family. There was as much focus on fun as on ministry in those days. Second, unity rooted in a trust for each other began to change the collective attitude of the church. When he arrived, Greg described the church as "the most defeated group of people I have ever encountered." Slowly, hope replaced that defeat. The dream that God had birthed in Chesterton Church of the Nazarene was still alive. The people of Duneland believed they were called to be good news for people who were worn out, frustrated, or feeling neglected by religion. They wanted to be pioneers, sowing seeds in hard soil and bringing about a kingdom harvest in unexpected places. (In a beautiful demonstration of God's humor and provision, this pioneering congregation was eventually able to purchase the entire building that had been the home of Pioneer Lumber.)

The visioning process reaffirmed their commitment to being innovators, but it also reinforced one major issue that had plagued Duneland since its launch. No one had any idea *how* to be the church they felt called to be. No one had ever been in a church like the one they imagined. No one had any training or education in being that kind of church. No one was even sure they had *seen* that kind of church. On a Tuesday night as they sat in their converted warehouse and met with the district superintendent to do a two-year review of Greg's leadership, they experienced a pivotal moment of clarity.

Pastor Greg asked the catalyzing question: "I am so excited about this vision we have. I can give myself to this vision. The only problem is that I don't know how to lead us there. Do any of you know how to become this kind of church? If so, tell me what to do, and I will do it."

The stunned silence that followed told the story. Although they had clarity on who they wanted to be, Duneland had no map for how to get there. It was a brand-new destination for all of them. They were willing to be pioneers, but they would need some guides. Thankfully, right around that same time, God connected them with some amazing guides to lead the process.

Helpful Resources for Visioning

Auxano, a church-consulting agency, specializes in helping churches discover and articulate their unique vision. The Duneland Community church board worked with Auxano and read *Church Unique*, by Auxano founder Will Mancini to help them discover a new vision. Auxano was able to help them reach beyond platitudes to describe the unique mission to which God was calling Duneland: "Cultivating God's Wholeness in a Broken World."

Cultivating Missional Change

At a district event two weeks later, leaders from Duneland encountered the organization 3D Movements. Birthed out of St. Thomas Crookes Church in Sheffield, England, 3DM specializes in helping churches learn how to build cultures that produce disciples that make other disciples and live as extended families of mission. Duneland, buoyed by a missional development grant from their district, committed to three years in what 3DM calls a learning community. This process gave feet to their vision and enabled them to intentionally shape their culture in ways that would lead to missional innovation.

The process, of course, was anything but linear. Armed with a clear sense of calling and communally confessed ignorance, Duneland began the difficult work of creating a culture of innovation. They knew from the beginning that it would take a lot of trial and error to experience the kind of breakthrough they sought. The process began first with two years of leadership development. After those two years, the leaders who had been trained and equipped began to go out and lead others. After three years of shaping this culture, there still wasn't much obvious fruit to show for it in regard to mission, but there was significant spiritual fruit in the lives of the leaders. Then the journey got much more fun.

In order to discover how to live out their mission in their context, Duneland began to try a little bit of everything. They hosted coat and hat drives for local schools, school supply drives for local church planters, chili cook-offs to collect canned goods and raise money for the local food pantry, Angel Tree to provide Christmas gifts for families of inmates, and Operation Christmas Child to send gifts overseas. Each missional activity was a chance for the church to practice and learn. Some things went really well while other experiments were minor successes—at best.

One of Duneland's greatest missional struggles was finding partners in ministry. Duneland knew they needed partners to help lead them into their mission and bridge the gap between where they were and where

---

Learn More

Read about the church that launched 3DM in chapter 6: "The Church That Launched a Global Movement."

they wanted to be. Locally, they tried partnerships with the Boys and Girls Club, the YMCA, a young adult drug rehabilitation center, local schools, and other churches. None of these were great successes. Some flopped entirely. Instead of taking their failures as a sign that they were doing the wrong thing, Duneland instead reflected on and learned from every experiment.

They learned that ministry was most effective when they encountered individuals who already wanted to partner with them. When Duneland tried to force their way in or go places where the door wasn't open very wide, things went poorly. For them, relationships needed to precede partnerships. They also learned that partnerships and ministry went best when they were first rooted in the passion of the congregation, not the passion of the pastor. When one of the laity heard the call of God and shared that passion with others, the response was far greater than when the invitation came from the pulpit.

Finally, after trying a little bit of everything, breakthrough happened in the most unexpected way: brassieres. Yes, that is right. The missional breakthrough Duneland had been working for all these years centered around bras—lots and lots of bras.

For several years, Pastor Greg had served on the board of a nonprofit organization called Free the Girls (freethegirls.org). Free the Girls provides jobs for survivors of sex trafficking around the globe by collecting new and slightly used bras from all over the world. The bras are sorted and shipped to their partners in Mozambique, Uganda, and El Salvador. There, women who have been rescued from slavery and trafficking are trained to run their own business—selling used bras in the clothing market. It is truly remarkable how effective selling bras actually is for ending the cycle of poverty and empowering these amazing women to build new lives for themselves. As Free the Girls began to grow, some of the women in the Duneland church grew interested in the cause and the fight against human trafficking. One leader in particular, Pam Gumns, hosted her own bra drive and got actively involved. The number of laypeople who wanted to know more and find out how to get involved created a buzz within the church. At first, people were somewhat uncomfortable talking about bras and sex trafficking at church. Over time, their discomfort gave way to a strong passion for justice.

Remember the rented warehouse? After a few years of tenancy, Duneland began to feel at home. They had been holding twelve acres of property on the edge of town, reserved as the site of their new build-

THE CHURCH OF ACCIDENTAL ABOLITIONISTS

ing some time in the far distant future. Instead, they sold the land and bought the warehouse they had been renting when God made it clear that their future was in the old lumberyard, which was far cheaper, much more visible from the highway, and perfectly functional. It *also* had lots of storage space. Somewhat out of the blue, Free the Girls contacted Greg and asked if the church would be willing to be the shipping and receiving site for all the bras being sent around the globe. Up to that point, Free the Girls had received about 75,000–100,000 bras. Greg immediately agreed because this was just what Duneland had been praying for: a long-term ministry partner. The warehouse they were on the verge of purchasing would be an incredible home for the bra ministry. It had garage doors, access for forklifts, and a recycling center for all the boxes. The warehouse also housed a congregation that had spent several years trying out anything and everything they could, just waiting for a new mission.

The response to the question of becoming "the bra church," as the local community began to refer to Duneland, was immediate and enthusiastic. As soon as Greg got the invitation to partner with Free the Girls, he called Pam and asked her to head up the entire ministry. Within six months Duneland was working every day of the week in partnership with Free the Girls, learning to be abolitionists in the fight against human trafficking. This partnership turned into a missional snowball effect. Not only was Duneland engaged in a beautifully creative ministry, but it also became the partner other organizations had been looking for. Over the next several years, Free the Girls would help inspire partnerships with the Boys and Girls Club, Zonta groups, Soroptimist groups, schools, universities, churches, and other Nazarene districts. Those who wanted to become abolitionists found in Duneland willing and ready partners, prepared to lead the way.

Tasting new life by joining in with God's work in the world awakened a hunger within the Duneland church. Suddenly, many were ready to try their hands at almost anything missional. One unremarkable Sunday in January, a representative of World Vision, Rusty Funk, made a simple, three-minute presentation. He shared about the amazing work of providing clean water across the globe. Rusty's job is to help people get involved in that work by fundraising. All of that is fairly normal, except that Team World Vision's primary vehicle for fundraising is to get people to run marathons. When Rusty asked to visit Duneland, Greg was quick to agree, but he offered a word of caution. He knew the church would think World Vision was awesome, but there weren't more than a couple of people in the church who had ever run a marathon. He doubted Rusty would gain much traction.

The appeal was simple. Rusty walked to the front of the church carrying an old, plastic canister filled with water. As he deposited the can on the stage, everyone could hear the sloshing of the water moving back and forth. Then Rusty talked about how, every day, all over the world, women and children walk four or five miles to fill a plastic container just like that one with dirty water. The daily pursuit of water means they can't work or go to school, which puts them in danger of falling into trafficking. The dirty water makes them sick and keeps them weak. All of these dangers and risks are things we can do something about. It only takes about fifty dollars to provide clean water for one person for ten to twenty years.

Rusty then invited anyone who was interested to stay after the service to learn how they could make a difference. Astoundingly, 30 people stayed afterward to hear about running a marathon. Ten months later, 15 of those people ran the Chicago marathon. Fourteen of those 15 people were first-time marathoners. Together, the group raised enough money to provide clean water for more than 400 people. A few years earlier, Duneland could barely muster the energy to hold a worship service, but now 15 adults had radically altered their lives to run a marathon. The next year, there were a dozen new and several return runners. Over the next 3 years, more than 30 percent of the adults at Duneland would run the Chicago marathon to provide clean water in Africa. All told, they raised more than $60,000 in that time, providing clean water for more than 1,200 people. This was unexpected, beautiful, world-changing fruit, birthed out of a people who had learned to dream bigger dreams and step out in faith.

Becoming an Innovating People

With each breakthrough of faith, a new boldness emerged among the people of Duneland Community Church. If they could serve trafficking survivors around the globe, what could they do locally? A group of leaders, having learned from their earlier missional ventures, got together for a year of discernment about local trafficking issues. They knew they were called to do something, but they didn't know where to start. For a year, they worked slowly and prayerfully through International Justice Mission's curriculum called *Community Justice Assessment Tool for Churches* to discern the needs of their local area, what was already happening to

To learn more about how your church can work for justice in your community, check out the International Justice Mission's local *Community Justice Assessment Tool for Churches*: https://www.ijm.org/content /local-community-justice-assessment-tool.

meet those needs, where the gaps were, and how Duneland's strengths intersected with those needs.

Once again the starting posture was one of confessed ignorance, certainty of calling, and willingness to learn. Over the year of discernment, they learned as much as they could about the area. Human trafficking in northwest Indiana and the Chicagoland area is very different than Mozambique or El Salvador. Conversations with local judges, sheriffs, nonprofit organizations, and even the FBI yielded significant insight into the trafficking issues of their region. They spent time with those already doing anti-trafficking work in other locations around the country. Most importantly, for a year, they didn't do anything more than meet together, learn, pray, and research.

As they engaged in mission, they did so in small ways. Education and sharing what they had learned was a low-challenge entry into the fight against human trafficking. Then there were field trips. They went out with others working the streets of Chicago to minister to prostitutes. Next, it was a field trip to Indianapolis to visit women in strip clubs with a ministry called Strip Free. These trips were a bit more challenging. When people commit themselves to obeying the call of God, they rarely imagine that means walking the streets of Chicago at 2:00 a.m. sharing the love of Christ with prostitutes or bringing gifts to exotic dancers in strip clubs. Once you get a taste for this kind of mission, however, you realize that the call of God can lead to almost anything.

The lessons from Duneland's story, reaching all the way back to its founding as Chesterton Church of the Nazarene, are rooted in the tangible process of learning to dream. Dreaming feels like an ethereal idea, not a concrete process. Duneland's story, though, is all about the hands-on work of cultivating. Each success and failure was a hands-on experience in learning about the faithfulness of God and God's ability to use anyone for any purpose. If a group of ordinary Christians, in a small-town bubble, gathering in a church that had never thrived, can end up meeting in a lumberyard, running marathons, becoming known to the surrounding community as the bra church, and visiting strip clubs—then certainly God can bring about resurrection anywhere.

Learn More

http://www.dunelandchurch.org

https://3dmovements.com

auxano.com

https://freethegirls.org

Greg's blog: https://holinessreeducation.com

Josh's blog: http://www.humblefuture.com

"The Preaching Life: An Interview with Josh Broward," NTS Center for Pastoral Leadership, https://cpl.nts.edu/index.php/resources/ministry/item/351-the-preaching-life-interview-with-josh-broward

Susan Emery, "Church Packs Bras to Fight Sex Trafficking," *NW Indiana Times* (June 11, 2013), http://www.nwitimes.com/news/local/porter/duneland/chesterton/church-packs-bras-to-fight-sex-trafficking/article_0cc8538e-a5dd-5c9b-b31a-54bf3506e265.html

Recommended Resources

Church Unique: How Missional Leaders Cast Vision, Capture Culture, and Create Movement, by Will Mancini (2008)

God Dreams: 12 Vision Templates for Finding and Focusing Your Church's Future, by Will Mancini and Warren Bird (2016)

Discussion Questions

1. Has your church experienced anything similar to Duneland's first sixty years of quiet, hidden existence?

2. What are the biggest crises your church has faced? How have those crises changed your church?

3. When Duneland finally settled on their vision, they realized they didn't know how to do it. When have you faced something similar?

4. Outside consultants were key for Duneland's process of discerning their vision and learning how to fulfill it. Has your church ever experimented with consultants? How do you think you should go about finding the right kind of consultant for your church?

5. Duneland's partnership with Free the Girls launched them into the fight against sex trafficking on both global and local levels, but this work carries with it an edgy discomfort. What are your thoughts on whether discomfort is inherent in deep, missional work? When have you felt God calling you to do something really uncomfortable?

6. The International Justice Mission's *Community Justice Assessment Tool for Churches* was helpful for Duneland to understand where their strengths intersected with their community's needs. How could your church do a needs assessment for your community?

6

The Church That Launched a Global Movement

Name: St. Thomas Crookes

Denomination: Church of England

Location: Sheffield, England

Size: Mega (2,500)

Ethnic Makeup: 68% Caucasian; 15% International students; 10% Iranian; 5% Black British (and Nigerian); 2% Chinese

—m—

"As we look around as Christendom is crumbling and the landscape of the church is forever changed, a stark revelation emerges: Most of us have been trained and educated for a world that no longer exists."
—Mike Breen, former pastor of St. Thomas Crookes[1]

—m—

When our rapidly changing world makes us feel inadequate, unprepared, and unmoored, our normal response is fear. For some, however, this topsy-turvy world provides a wonderful excuse to break free of normal modes of operation and do some experimenting. The rapidly changing cultural dynamics of the twenty-first century have afforded many churches the necessary permission to think outside the proverbial box. If the North American church wants to peer into its future and discover pioneers who have already been confronting these challenges, it should look to Europe. There, Christendom has been in decline over the last century. Many great cathedrals of Europe now serve not as houses of worship but as museums, tourist attractions, and even apartment buildings. Great cities that birthed world-changing Christian movements are now ripe fields for mission, with fewer practicing Christians than Muslims. So when something remarkable takes place—such as when a global Christian movement emerges from a post-industrial, post-Christian city in England—the rest of the church should take notice and learn.

Sheffield, England, is a town steeped in history. Historical records and archaeological evidence prove that the area has been used by humans for thousands of years. It has been part of British history since before the Romans, the Danes, and the Normans. Christianity has been present in this area for more than a thousand years. The church has a sense of permanence there. All of Sheffield's history, for the past thousand years, is woven throughout the presence of the church.[2]

More than 50 percent of the population in the United Kingdom still identifies as Christian, but only 4–5 percent actually attend a church service in any given week.[3] The church there faces numerous challenges that are increasingly familiar in the North American context. Religious identification is rooted in culture, not active faith. Congregations are rapidly aging and dwindling. The fastest-growing groups are those who identify as nonreligious. The church is seen as part of the past, not part of the present—much less the future. So how did this town, where the church is in sharp decline, give birth to a church whose influence has stretched around the globe?

In many ways, the story reflects the industrial history of Sheffield. In the eighteenth and nineteenth centuries, Sheffield became a world-renowned center of manufacturing. In particular, innovations in the production of steel and cutlery helped its rise to prominence. Over the years Sheffield has remained a world leader in manufacturing because of ongoing innovations. New metallurgy and manufacturing techniques, developed in Sheffield, have radically changed the process of steelmaking. In similar ways, the St. Thomas Church of Sheffield became a worldwide force of church renewal and kingdom breakthrough because of a culture of innovation.

St. Thomas Anglican Parish was originally formed in the 1840s to serve a growing rural population outside of Sheffield, in the village of Crookes. In the 1970s, the innovations that would shape the future of the church began. This Anglican parish merged with Crookes Baptist Church and began to invest in youth ministry. With the merger came a renewed season of growth and ministry development within the church. The real change, however, came with a movement of the Spirit in the 1980s. A Spirit-empowered revival, influenced by Vineyard leader John Wimber, began to shape this Anglican-Baptist church into something new altogether. An increased focus on the Spirit was accompanied by breakthroughs in worship and evangelism. St. Thomas began to inno-vate in significant ways with their worship experience. In particular, a gathering called the Nine O'Clock Service had a dramatic effect on their ability to connect with young adults who had previously checked out of Christianity.

Following these decades of experimentation and openness to become something different, the church really found its footing under the leader-ship of Pastor Mike Breen in the 1990s. Mike is a gifted leader whose skills and calling fall under the biblical role of apostle. He is by nature and gift-ing a spiritual fire starter, an entrepreneur, someone willing to take great risks for the kingdom. The work he began in Sheffield has led him all over the world as a teacher, trainer, and movement starter. The culture that Mike helped create at St. Thomas was unique in several ways.

First, in order to better accomplish their mission of reaching a people surrounded by the ghosts of the church, they had to train up and send out missionaries. Rather than rethinking how they could try to attract the uninterested to their church, they began to focus on how they could send their people out into the lives of the uninterested—materializing in an intensive focus on discipleship. Specifically, they began to train their people to be disciples who make disciples. They moved the power of evangelism and discipleship back to the priesthood of believers and removed those tasks from the sole domain of clergy.

Second, they began to experiment with new forms of church commu-nity that would be new entry points into the church. Instead of gathering in large groups, they sent people out to build extended families. These mid-sized groups of twenty to fifty people, called missional communities, would become compelling havens for those in need of good news. They formed in homes, in neighborhood gathering spots, at sports fields, and in bars. They formed around shared activities, geography, needs, or simply friendship.

This movement out into the community resulted in unbelievable kingdom breakthrough. Over time, hundreds and hundreds of religiously uninterested or irreligious people surrendered their lives to Christ. Over the next decade, this movement of kingdom transformation, rooted in discipleship and missional communities, would move from St. Thomas out across the United Kingdom, greater Europe, and across the globe. It would become a global movement connecting churches and Christians from a wide array of tribes and nations. Of course, the story isn't that simple. This breakthrough was the result of hard work, lots of failure, great sacrifice, and huge leaps of faith.

Learning from Embarrassing Failure

When Mike Breen arrived at St. Thomas, the church was in the throes of a great failure. The Nine O'Clock Service, one of the first postmodern worship experiments, had grown to the point that it had become its own church. With a gifted and charismatic leader, it became the beloved poster child for the future of the Anglican Church. Unfortunately, the great freedom given to the Nine O'Clock Service wasn't matched by great accountability. The service and the church it became crashed and burned in spectacular fashion. This was a failure of such significance that it became the subject of news reports and documentaries.

So, as Mike began to move the church forward in greater exploration of its mission, he was doing so with a congregation that had experienced the dark side of innovation (see chapter 13). It had risked, won, and then eventually lost big. The significant growth and movement of the Spirit they had enjoyed was but short-lived. Like a plant that grows suddenly and then withers in the sun, the new ground taken for the kingdom in Sheffield was quickly lost.

Determined to continue taking new ground, the team at St. Thomas created a culture that not only allowed for trying new things *and* allowed for failure, but it was also a culture that was rooted in deep relationship. The accountability of small discipleship groups, shared leadership, and extended families on mission allowed them to foster a culture of low

> **Leadership Insight**
>
> One of the keys for a culture of innovation is high accountability but low control. Cultivating this empowering environment takes time and significant relational development.

control and high accountability. Setting up camp in the land of deep relationship, intentional leadership development, low control, and high accountability enabled St. Thomas to move into a life of sustained innovation. There was a shift away from success according to the world's standards and a shift toward the biblical idea of fruitfulness (John 15). Obedience doesn't always lead to the quantifiable, measurable results we want. But God promises that he is in charge of fruitfulness; we are in charge of obedience. By focusing on understanding God's call, the people of St. Thomas were able to devote themselves fully to the pursuit of fruitfulness. They trusted that, if God wanted to make them successful, God would do so. But fruitfulness born of obedience was their goal.

It was clear to the team at St. Thomas that obedience required them to be a church that made disciples who would make disciples. They became a center of training and leadership development by raising up disciples and teaching them to lead others. Of course, though, if we focus on leadership development and reproduction, there will be failures. In a discipling and reproducing culture, we send out those who are inexperienced to do the work of the kingdom, just as Jesus did when he first sent out the Twelve (Luke 9) and then sent out the seventy-two (Luke 10). Developing new generations of leaders requires us to put people in positions of responsibility while they are still learning. This is over and against the practice of waiting until people are experts. In a culture focused on success, we put experts in leadership positions, and we keep them there for a long time—until they fail, quit, or retire. But St. Thomas learned to put people into leadership who were still in training, even when there may have been more experienced people available.

Innovative Leadership Development in Action

To understand the culture of St. Thomas and how they identified, equipped, and empowered everyday people to live out the mission of God, one need look no further than Paul Maconochie. When Mike arrived at St. Thomas, Paul was a twenty-four-year-old teacher and volunteer music worship leader. Paul watched as Mike led the church in a new direction. The church's focus was shifting to the new missional communities. Additionally, they were innovating new ways of discipling and training their leaders. Some in the church rejected this new vision, but Paul was inspired and compelled to join the mission.

Filled with excitement, passion, and undoubtedly some naiveté, Paul and his wife, Heloise, decided to lead their own missional community. They went to their music team, consisting of about thirty talented musicians, and shared their vision for the team to become a community that practiced hospitality and welcomed strangers into their lives. They would take their musical worship and make it a lifestyle by inviting those who would never step foot into a worship service to come be a part of their extended family. The suggestion was met with a robust rejection. Out of their team of thirty, only three stayed to form the new missional community. Paul was sure that Mike would be furious that he had so quickly blown up his music team. Instead, Mike just encouraged him to keep going.

Imagine their shock as the music team went from a full band of gifted musicians to a keyboardist, a guitarist, and an oboist. Paul was not overflowing with joy or confidence with this inauspicious beginning. Despite their small start and the awkward worship sets featuring the oboe, they pressed on. They began to study what it meant to welcome people into their lives. More importantly, they began to practice welcoming strangers into their lives and their fellowship. This team of willing experimenters became quick learners. Soon their gatherings were filled with drug addicts, broken people, the spiritually uninterested, and a host of others.

Within 18 months, they had grown to about 120 people, multiplying into 3 groups of about 40 people each. Those others groups, led by people Paul and Heloise mentored, grew and thrived as well. Around 45 people became Christians during this time. In a town where only 2–3 percent of the population have an active faith in Christ, this is tremendous success. Just as noteworthy, this dynamic movement of God was being led by unassuming, everyday Christians. They had simply learned to be obedient to the call of God by welcoming those around them into their lives. They didn't allow their initial failures to derail their faithfulness or stop their mission. They just kept working on being obedient and trusted that God would lead them to fruitfulness.

Paul felt a new calling on his life as he led the missional community groups. He approached the staff at St. Thomas and shared his sense of calling to pursue full-time ministry and join the staff. The church, which was learning this delicate process of raising up and empowering leaders, told him to continue leading missional communities. As Paul led, they watched and weighed his calling. Paul was able to grow a significant ministry within the waters of St. Thomas, so they were eventually confident in his calling. His leadership capacity had been tested, and then his faith was tested. St. Thomas invited Paul to join the staff two days a week—without pay. He attended seminary as a part-time student while he volunteered for St. Thomas.

Paul's test of faith was rewarded when the church began to experience a new surge of power that allowed them to break into some hard-to-reach areas. Paul was a big part of this new movement. Eventually St. Thomas planted into a new venue, based in the building of a famously hedonistic nightclub called The Roxy. Paul was asked to lead one of the services there. Suddenly, this one-time schoolteacher was preaching every other week to about four hundred people, most of them older than him and stubbornly irreligious. (Keep in mind that four hundred people is a large Anglican parish in this part of the world.)

By all accounts, Paul was thrust into a role that was beyond his experience, but the church had witnessed within him a great capacity for leadership. Along with preaching, Paul was also responsible for overseeing about eight or nine missional communities. At The Roxy, Paul was thrown into the deep end and learned to lead with hands-on experience. The church didn't wait until he was an expert. Instead, they tested his calling, mentored him, discipled him, and gave him vital, frontline leadership experience. This investment into Paul—who had quickly transformed from a twenty-four-year-old schoolteacher and volunteer music worship leader into a significant missional leader—would prove vitally important over the next few years.

Leadership Insight

Innovation requires buy-in from those you lead. You are better off with three sold-out leaders than thirty who aren't truly committed to the vision.

Innovation Replication

In 2004, Mike Breen left St. Thomas. He felt called to take what he had learned and train leaders in the United States, where he eventually formed 3D Movements (introduced in chapter 5). In the wake of Mike's departure, Paul became the leader of St. Thomas. This was a pivotal moment for the church—one that tested their culture and mission. Under Mike's apostolic leadership, St. Thomas had become one of the most significant churches in all of Great Britain. Their efficacy in raising up and reproducing disciples was bringing about a great harvest in their post-Christian context. Mike's powerful personal presence was undoubtedly part of what made St. Thomas such a place of innovation.

For many movements, the moment when the dynamic and gifted leader leaves is the moment when the story begins to change for the worse. It is difficult to fill the personality vacuum of such a charismatic leader. This task seemed especially daunting for now thirty-three-year-old Paul Maconochie as he took over leadership of the church. The membership of the main congregation of the downtown plant of St. Thomas, now called St. Thomas Philadelphia after the area of Sheffield where it was based, was around 1,200 at this time. This made it a huge congregation for their context, and at thirty-three, Paul was considered an especially young senior leader. However, St. Thomas had established a culture of releasing people for ministry, young leaders especially, and they were prepared to entrust their future to the next generation.

St. Thomas had a new campus and a great leadership team. It looked like the transition would go smoothly, and they installed Paul as the new senior leader with great confidence that all they had built would continue to thrive. Once Mike left, however, a lot of people followed him out the door. Over the next three years, more than four hundred people left the church. Paul and others began to wonder how he could possibly step into the role that Mike had filled. A lot of the high-level staff and lay leaders walked out the door and took with them a lot of the resources and financial backing the church relied upon. Within three years of Mike's exodus-causing departure, only one of the eight senior staff members remained at the church. This was a dark and difficult time for St. Thomas—a time that challenged the culture of innovation and leadership development they had created. The loss of so much influence and so many resources threatened to derail the kingdom movement that had begun in Sheffield.

Leadership Insight

The transition of leadership from one generation to the next is often where vision goes to die. This is especially true with pioneering leaders and innovators. If they do not spend time teaching the next generation to do what they have done, innovation will cease.

The season was also very difficult for Paul in particular. Any leader who endures a season of such significant loss and struggle will take it personally. The stress can absolutely eat you alive. Paul was no different, and the physical toll ended up putting him in the hospital. Part of his recovery required him to take six months off from work. During his time of rest and abiding, God spoke to Paul about the type of leader Paul was called to be. God hadn't called him to be Mike Breen. It was time for Paul to learn how to lead St. Thomas as himself, not trying to be someone else. Paul is unassuming, down to earth, and seems very much like an average guy (or bloke). He doesn't have the charismatic persona we often picture at the head of a movement. But beneath his quiet exterior was a leader perfectly gifted to lead this church at this moment.

By the time Paul returned to leadership, there were significant struggles in the church. Only about 50 percent of church members were participating in missional communities, down from about 90 percent under Mike. They were down four hundred people in regular worship. However, they retained their most significant strength: a culture that had learned how to develop leaders and send them out in mission. They weren't starting out with a bare cupboard. They resisted the temptation to chase after what they had been. When they had to replace the senior leaders who left, they decided to raise up leaders from within instead of hiring the best experts they could find from the outside. The strength of who they were as a church was not concentrated in one dynamic leader; rather, it lay in an empowered leadership pipeline that was taking everyday people, like Paul, and turning them into disciples.

So they looked around their church to see whom they already had. Who was ready to grow and be shaped for a larger leadership role? This attitude was crucial for what was to come. The next generation of leaders they would raise up, under Paul, would go on to bring about an unbelievable amount of fruitfulness and innovation, and it started by looking at what they had rather than chasing what they had lost.

One such leader was found in an unlikely spot. Paul noticed that they had a gifted young leader named Pete James already on their staff; it just so happened that he was a janitor. St. Thomas invested in this volunteer leader, a.k.a. church janitor, and within the next decade, Pete James would become not only a tremendous worship leader but also a trainer of other worship leaders across the country.

Another great leader was discovered in Rich Robinson, a children's worker. Investment into Rich resulted in growth within the children's ministry and also in Rich's professional growth to be a church-wide leader. Rich began his ministry leading an evangelistic kids' club in an urban neighborhood. He was part of a team of five leaders trying to innovate new ministries to children. They had both great success and significant struggles. As the club grew, it became a fuller ministry that included youth and families. The team of five young adults, however, could not maintain all these levels of ministry and relationships, and the club eventually plateaued.

The team realized their ministry was limited in its capacity because they were not equipped to do all they were trying to do. This struggle would ultimately serve as a catalyst for Rich's development as a leader. Faced with these challenges, Rich and his team learned new ways to lead their ministry, they grew in their personal capacity, and they broke through the barriers that had caused their plateau. Rich took on expanded leadership in the church and began to lead the Youth & Kids ministry. Having learned from their experiments, they didn't plant a kids' club unless there was an intentional strategy for youth ministry to go alongside it. They also made sure they had people moving into the neighborhood to live incarnationally alongside the clubs. Rich continued to develop, and slowly he moved into other leadership roles in the church. In time, Rich would become the leader of 3D Movements in Europe (3DM Europe). This network of churches began to teach other churches how to cultivate the culture of missional discipleship that had been pioneered in Sheffield.

In their youth department, St. Thomas identified Rich Atkinson. During his stay in the hospital and his time recovering, God spoke to Paul directly about Rich. Although Rich was loosely connected to the church, Paul and Rich didn't really know each other. But God told Paul to hire Rich and to unleash him as a leader for their youth ministry. Coming in as a new leader, Rich was amazed at how liberating Paul was. There was a lot of internal pressure on the youth ministry within the church. It wasn't thriving. It would have been easy for Paul to give in to that pressure and hire an expert. Instead, being obedient to God, he hired a young leader with the right heart and gave him the freedom to chase after God. In the first conversation Paul had with Rich, he told him, "God has called you here. Don't feel any pressure. Just go for it. Follow where God is calling you. Don't hold back; just go and give it a try." There were no golden calves. Rich had permission to change anything if it led them closer to where God was calling them.

This unusual hire and immense freedom yielded stunning results. Within four years, their youth ministry had grown to more than nine hundred youth. The youth made up more than 50 percent of the church. Working through a model of low-maintenance, low-production, decentralized ministry groups, they experienced a level of breakthrough with youth that St. Thomas had never before seen. Instead of creating a youth ministry dependent on experts, they created a youth ministry in which the average person believed they could be successful. Rich said, "The simpler our groups became, the more successful they became. The average person looked at what we were doing and thought, *Well, even I can do that.*" Their models were simple, and they stayed intentionally small. They actively worked toward reproduction, and they allowed for innovation through failure. When any given youth leader raised the production level too high, to a level that would be difficult for less-skilled volunteers to replicate, Rich told them it was "too awesome" and that they needed to simplify again.

Rich knew they were really doing something amazing when he visited one of their missional communities and met some of the students. One of the students asked him, "Who are you?"

Rich responded, "I'm your youth leader!"

The student looked at him with a puzzled expression and said, "No, you're not; he is."

It was true. Even though Rich was organizing and leading this vibrant youth ministry, he had successfully raised up another generation of leaders who were doing the groundbreaking work on the frontlines. The end result is a church with more than 50 percent of its congregation under 25 years of age. This is what investing in the future looks like.

St. Thomas became so successful at training up leaders to do youth ministry that others came to them for training. Eventually Rich started Rebuild, a ministry that trains and equips youth and young adult ministry leaders. He became an influential voice, training leaders across the UK and Europe.

Another great leadership story involved Peter Findlay. Peter was the senior leader at a church in Coventry, England. Their church became part of a network of churches that shared life and ministry together. Paul invested in Peter and these other leaders, helping them through the process of changing their culture. Paul discipled and trained these other senior leaders and helped them reproduce themselves in others. Peter marvels that today in Coventry there are two and three generations of leaders who look like Paul. They lead like Paul. They have inherited this leadership model because Peter learned to lead like Paul, and then he reproduced that in the leaders. This is all the more striking because none of those leaders have ever met Paul. Later, when Paul felt called to come the United States to participate in 3DM's leadership development movement, Peter was the one who replaced him in Sheffield. The church was able to bring in a leader who already understood their culture and was able to help them protect and maintain it.

All of these breakthroughs would lead to a level of fruitfulness during the ten years of Paul's tenure as the senior leader of St. Thomas that matched or exceeded the fruit of the previous time under the leadership of Mike Breen. This fruitfulness was the product of a culture that produced innovation by growing, training, and releasing leaders in very intentional ways. They allowed for failure, gave the keys to leadership over to young leaders, built deep, relational accountability, and trusted that obedience to God would yield results. The story of St. Thomas is so uniquely powerful that it is well worth pausing to consider some of the major characteristics of this culture, started by Mike Breen and expanded by Paul Maconochie:

- There is far more power in having a movement full of leaders who have a vision they are pursuing than in having an organization full of volunteers following one leader's vision.
- Discipleship without reproduction is unhealthy and unbiblical.
- You must release your leaders to lead, even when they aren't quite ready.
- Failure can always prepare us for success if failure is used to learn.
- You protect your organizational culture by reproducing leaders internally.
- Often the most significant innovations happen in the second and third generations of leaders.

Leadership Insight

When you obediently sow seeds of grace in great abundance, especially when it doesn't directly benefit your ministry, you will reap a harvest in the most unexpected places.

Sheffield, England, seems an unlikely place for a global movement of the church to begin. It has all the disadvantages you can imagine to experience a revival. Perhaps it was the difficulty of having so many odds stacked against them that gave their leaders the courage to fail. A commitment to innovation, a host of failures large and small, and the difficult work of cultivating leaders have given birth to a remarkable growth of the kingdom. It gives us hope that, if the kingdom can break through in Sheffield, we can foster similar quantum leaps in other hard-to-reach areas.

Learn More

- https://stthomascrookes.org
- http://ncsheffield.org
- https://3dmovements.com
- http://www.michaeljamesbreen.com

Recommended Resources, all by Mike Breen and the 3DM Team

- *Building a Discipling Culture* (2011)
- *Multiplying Missional Leaders* (2012)
- *Leading Missional Communities* (2013)
- *Launching Kingdom Movements* (2013)

Discussion Questions

1. St. Thomas Crookes Church has experienced several waves each of great breakthroughs and painful defeats. Which is closer to where your church is now? How does this make you feel—hopeful, discouraged, afraid?

2. Church leaders rarely tell their followers to make something "less awesome," but that was a critical step for multiplying St. Thomas's youth ministry. Does your church think or work for multiplication of your ministries? If so, how? If not, how might you start thinking in that way?

3. The St. Thomas story is really a story of leadership multiplication. Who is investing into your leadership? In whom are you investing?

4. St. Thomas raised up leaders from within. Who at your church or in your organization might be ready for more leadership responsibility?

5. This church gave young leaders great leeway, both to experiment and to fail as part of the learning process—with high accountability and low control. How can your church cultivate this freedom? How can you empower leaders who might not have adequate experience yet but who might be able to grow into their roles?

7

The Church That Stopped Hiding from the Neighbors

Name: Leonardtown

Denomination: Church of the Nazarene

Location: Leonardtown, Maryland

Size: Medium (120)

Ethnic Mix: 75% Caucasian; 13% Black; 12% Samoan

THE SETTING is the epitome of the "church on the square." The century-old church building is classic Americana: prominent steeple, stained-glass windows, and steps leading up to the small porch and entrance. The Methodist congregation that built the facility a hundred years ago moved out in the late 1980s. They relocated to a newer, easy-maintenance building with appealing features for the young families moving into the Washington, DC area. Now, as Leonardtown Church of the Nazarene, this small-town church seems to shine with all the best of the past as they rise to the challenge of relevance and fruitfulness in the present.

With 3,500 residents, Leonardtown rests quietly on the lower end of the peninsula formed by the Patuxent River as it flows into Chesapeake Bay. You would probably never see the town unless you were passing through on your way to somewhere else. The Mid-Atlantic district for the Church of the Nazarene planted Leonardtown Church of the Nazarene in the picturesque old building on the square in 1991, with some help from the nearby Hollywood Church of the Nazarene. (No, not that Hollywood. This one is only famous for being the home of Socks the Cat after the Clintons moved out of the White House.) In 1994, Paul MacPherson, a recent graduate of Nazarene Theological Seminary, made his way to the fledgling congregation in Leonardtown to begin his first assignment as a pastor.

During the first few years, the church was somewhat fragile and seemed unable to gather a critical mass of people who could invest the time and energy to bring a truly healthy congregation to birth. Through patient investment, Paul helped the small congregation mature, establish itself more securely, and find a beginning sense of identity in Leonardtown. In 2000 Paul left, feeling called to another church on a nearby district. For the next decade, the Leonardtown church labored on with relative stability but also with frequent struggles that kept them from making significant progress. After a series of pastoral turnovers, the church looked once again into a very uncertain future.

Homecoming and Open House

In 2011, the church faced the reality of its difficult situation. They were once again without a pastor, and they needed to discover a new way of being the church that would enable them to bear missional fruit in Leonardtown. In a fortuitous moment, members of the congregation heard that their former pastor, Paul MacPherson, might be available to resume his pastoral post. Within weeks, Paul returned to a discouraged but tenacious twelve people—who were hungry for a new sense of direction and mission.

One reason the original Methodist congregation had been so intent on moving away was the liability of their location on the aging town square. The old buildings around the square had been deteriorating, and several stood vacant for years. The county courthouse on the square was always busy—but not always in ways that were appealing. Residents of the nearby homes were selling and moving away, and the setting felt depressing to many.

By the time Paul arrived for his second tenure as pastor, however, the town had begun to revitalize the square. Buildings were remodeled, and new businesses moved in. To help reclaim their shared history, the city commissioned murals around the square—one next to the church parking lot. Most importantly, the downtown park became a regular venue for evening concerts, casual gatherings, and countywide events. An annual Christmas celebration was always held on the Saturday following Thanksgiving, and thousands of people gathered in the beautifully decorated square to watch the Christmas lights turn on for the season.

The previous Methodist congregation had been uneasy about gatherings in the park. Whenever the park was utilized for any public purpose, the church closed down to prevent vandalism or any other unnecessary intrusion. The newer Church of the Nazarene had carried forward this prioritization of privacy. This perspective began to change, however, as Paul and his small leadership team began to talk seriously about their mission and their location. The church building itself, with its ongoing repairs and limitations, had been a focus for several years. The congregation felt overwhelmed with maintaining the building, supporting a pastor, and participating financially in the denomination. For many years, survival was the only mission they could conceive. But Paul and a determined leadership team recognized that there was a larger mission that laid a higher-priority claim to their energy and resources.

Beginning with fervent prayer, they embarked on a collective soul search, asking the One who had called the church into being to lead them to a shared sense of mission and purpose. They came to believe that God was more interested in their survival than they were. They discovered that faithfulness demands much more than survival; they had to become involved in God's mission. After much prayer and discussion, they intentionally reoriented their church toward becoming a lively, welcoming presence on the town square. The church began with opening itself to new people, many of whom were young families moving into the wider community around Leonardtown. The renewed vitality of the town square began to attract people, and the church intentionally became more visible and engaged in the community.

The pastor began to cultivate relationships around town: visiting the county courthouse, offering to help wherever needed, and establishing deeply appreciated connections with town and county leadership. He became friends with business owners and frequented the new restaurants and cafés attracted to the newly developing area. The church established

Leadership Insight: Start with the Neighbors

If you aren't sure how to innovate in your context, you can start just by being a good neighbor. Get to know the residents, businesses, and organizations in closest proximity to your church's location. You don't have to start new activities to attract people. Just become an active participant in what is already going on. Do lots of listening and praying. See how you can help with the good things others have already begun. Don't go in with a mission to get conversions. Go in with a mission to be a good neighbor and to make new friends. Then look for open doors to deeper relationships. If you don't know where to start, just walk next door.

partnerships with nearby schools, assisting vulnerable children and providing weekend backpacks filled with nonperishable foods for children in need.

One of the most significant decisions was to embrace the opportunity provided by the thousands of people who gathered across the street for the annual Christmas festival. Rather than closing the doors and staying away, the congregation set up a living nativity scene on the small lawn and sidewalk in front of the church. They gave away gallons and gallons of hot chocolate and countless bags of popcorn, and they offered free, Christmas-themed face painting for the hundreds of children who milled around the town square with their parents.

The Innovation of Reclaiming Tradition

As they learned to be more involved in the community, the congregation discovered a new sense of mission. They worked for months to articulate their statement of mission: "Being the presence of Christ in our community." Then they used this statement regularly in their planning, in their developing relationships, and in incorporating new people into the life of the church.

The typical metrics are easy to quantify. The church grew from a Sunday gathering of 12 to 15 people to averaging more than 120. Most of this increase came from new believers. Other new people were church "dropouts," who had been disappointed and frustrated by churches.

As the church people began to develop more creative and relational connections with people outside the church, an unexpected response was their engagement with people who had been hurt by life—and often hurt by the institution of the church. Without judgment or criticism, the congregation began to open its arms to people who were wary and sometimes hostile toward the church, Christians, and religion in general. People who had previously felt shunned or rejected were given space to grieve, to criticize, or to react negatively when they were uncertain about the safety of this particular congregation. However, the loving hospitality and generous missionality of Leonardtown helped these people regain faith in the potential of Christian community. Through patient, gentle, loving concern, wounded people began to trust them. Soon the defenses came down as honest questions were discussed gently. Old hurts began to heal, enabling many to reclaim their home in God's family and grow in authentic relationship with Christ.

The church has also diversified beautifully, with African Americans and Samoans making up about 25 percent of the congregation. Leonardtown Church hopes to continue its growing diversity by building relationships in the town's growing Hispanic community in the near future. The congregation has also grown younger, moving from an average age of over 55 to around 35, with many children as well.

The old church building does not lend itself easily to a traditional Sunday school ministry. The few classrooms they have are very small. In many ways, this perceived limitation has actually freed the church to try other models of discipleship. The church does provide classes for young children on Sunday, but the remainder of the congregation meets in small groups throughout the week. Another inherent liability of being in an old building is its designation as a historic building. Any exterior repairs or improvements must comply with an established set of standards for consistency with the original form of the building and the neighborhood. These restrictions meant replacing a leaky old roof with an expensive new metal roof that complemented the original design.

Given the limitations of the building, the minimal activity and education space, and the limited parking, one might expect this growing congregation to consider options for a new location and more flexible facilities. However, at least for the foreseeable future, they see it as a matter of missional integrity that they remain on the town square. They feel a strong call to be active in their community and a redemptive and creative presence in the heart of their town. As new people began to discover the church, the congregation realized that something did need to change, though. As they began nearing a hundred regular attenders, the sanctuary became crowded beyond comfort. Because the church feels called to stay on the square, they added a second worship service to make room for the growing crowd. As the congregation looks ahead, they expect to continue adding more services rather than relocating to a larger facility.

As the size of the congregation has increased, so has their outreach into the community. They serve the homeless, visit a nearby prison, and host addiction-recovery ministries. Some of these folks have joined their faith family. The church also continues to engage their community through the downtown park. In addition to the living nativity at Christmas, they have also hosted a chili cook-off and public concerts by musicians from the church. Civic events always find the church an active and visible participant.

The Nazarenes in Leonardtown also began to expand their vision beyond their own context. Early on, as rapid growth began to occur, the church saw the need to look into the wider mission of God. Partnering with the York Stillmeadow Church of the Nazarene, a large church on their district, they established a relationship with Nazarenes on the East Jamaica district, which enabled Leonardtown to join York Stillmeadow in helping Jamaican churches improve their facilities and increase their outreach. After decades of isolation and fearing for their own future, Leonardtown Church was making a tangible difference on an international scale.

Patient Conversations, not Magic Bullets

One of the most common questions asked of Leonardtown Church of the Nazarene is, "What happened to you guys? How did a church that was struggling for survival move into a place of fruitfulness and community engagement that resulted in many new people coming to faith in Christ?"

The progress was slow but not accidental. This remarkable transformation is the result of hard work, fervent prayer, and honest and patient conversations. The pastor and the leadership team carefully listened for the voice of God and cultivated strategic planning for a different future. According to Paul, the real shift began when the church began to ask, "What is our mission?" Having zeroed in on the mission of being a faithful presence in Leonardtown, they began to ask how they could do that most effectively. There were no magic bullets, no marketable plans that brought the church to a new level of vitality and effectiveness. Together, they doggedly pursued faithfulness and openness to the Spirit's leading. The positive changes came through a simple determination to walk through the open doors and take risks that had no promise of success.

Much of the church's new mindset began with their involvement with the Gallup organization. Two Gallup tools were particularly helpful. The Faith Member Engagement survey helped them assess the spiritual engagement of their church family across a broad variety of factors. The StrengthsFinder survey enabled them to identify their particular resources as individuals and as a church. By this time, the church had already begun to grow, with about a third of the congregation becoming a part of the church within a space of two years. As a result of their work with Gallup, they began to foster spiritual growth by developing more spiritual intimacy with each other. They formed life groups and began to discuss their mission and their values as a congregation. God began to birth within them a genuine love for their community. They claimed the town of Leonardtown, especially the community immediately surrounding their church, as their Jerusalem (see Acts 1:8).

In his time at Leonardtown, Paul says he has learned that the primary responsibility for the church is to build kingdom citizens, not just members of a church. "I love the Church of the Nazarene," he said, "but my calling is to bring people into a kingdom relationship. We must create ministry that makes our people fervent believers who happen to be members of the Church of the Nazarene." To help cultivate a kingdom-minded culture, the church intentionally celebrates when an individual or a group has demonstrated the kingdom, whether that is helping someone embrace God's grace or helping a person in need.

Coping with the Challenges of Change

Paul understands personally the pitfalls and struggles of leading a church in a radically different direction. As the pastor and other key leaders moved Leonardtown Church toward more outward-focused ministry, that naturally meant less inward focus. During the first few months, the fear was tangible. The church was still in a struggle for survival, specifically regarding finances and attendance. Though the church had called Paul as their pastor with the clear awareness that he was free to help them rethink their future, it was not without resistance and fear among the few who were hanging in there. Some members, who had remained with the church through its most difficult days of uncertainty and vulnerability, greeted even vitally necessary changes with clenched fists and set jaws. Gradually, though, the congregation began to embrace the reality that, to move forward, the church needed to be willing to fail. It was obvious that the approaches of the first twenty years of the church's ministry had not produced a sustainable model for their future.

Another factor that gave the church permission to rethink their future was the MacPherson family's willingness to return to Leonardtown, knowing all their struggles and victories. "We are partners for the long haul," Paul assured them. As he demonstrated a patient persistence in leading them into new models of ministry, he influenced the core members, whose influence then spread outward into the church.

The district superintendent also gave the innovation process a stabilizing boost. He encouraged the church to experiment, to step outside the box, and to embrace creative ministry initiatives. He affirmed that innovative approaches would, by necessity, require a different kind of metric for determining the effectiveness of the church's unique ministry in its unique location. According to Paul, this support "from above" was one of the key ingredients for him to cultivate an atmosphere of innovation in the church. Because he wasn't afraid of abandonment or criticism, he could help remove those fears from the church environment as well.

Reflecting on the Process of Innovation

Leaders of the Leonardtown congregation understand that their church has undergone more than just physical renovations over the past several years. They have been in a process of conceptual innovation and missional restoration.

"I think our congregation understands that innovations are effective and worthwhile only when they are implemented with the express purpose of discipling and helping others grow in their relationship with our Lord," explained Maggie La Duca. "This just spills over into furthering the kingdom of heaven here on earth!"

"Innovations are necessary to keep up with the changing audience we wish to encounter as we meet our goal of 'being the presence of Christ in our community,'" Michael Stanley said. "Our church is committed to doing this through *relationships*, and we acknowledge that this is a complicated and stressful process."

Trenton Larrabee shared, "The growth of the church has not come from what we do but from who we have become. We have not targeted certain ministries, as such. People have developed a God-given passion for other people, and they started ministries living out those passions. It is not about any one person or program. It is about *being Christ* to our community because that is what we are!"

"One lesson that has constantly been hammered at me over the past couple of years, and one that we are learning still," reflects Eric Colvin, "is a reevaluation of what church is and should be. I think the final outcome will be that the method by which we do church will be innovation. We've learned a more Christlike method of evangelism—actually going to where the people are instead of waiting for them to come to us. Have we fully learned this lesson as a church? I don't think so, but I do think we are in the process of learning it. It will require some sacrifice of comfort, but that is probably a good thing."

Pastor Paul thinks the primary lesson they have learned is that all innovations need to be based on Scripture and flow organically out of who God has created them to be. Innovations must continually answer the question of how to carry out their mission of being the presence of Christ in their community, especially in the Leonardtown square. Leonardtown also learned that money is less important than mission. While financial resources are necessary to an extent, the primary need is people who are committed to the mission. Finances are more likely to follow the mission than to lead it. Once Leonardtown was living a compelling mission, their struggles with financial and organizational sustainability resolved naturally.

Perhaps the most important innovation in Leonardtown is simply reclaiming an incarnational mission that is rooted in the community directly around their church. With great intentionality, Leonardtown Church patiently and persistently reoriented themselves around the mission of God for their particular place and people. They understood that if any church is to make disciples of the nations, they must begin with their own neighbors.

A second critical piece of the innovative process is that the pastoral and lay leaders seriously engaged in a missional discernment process. They opened themselves to vulnerable conversations with God and with one another. They asked themselves who their neighbors are and how God wants them to love those neighbors. Together they discovered their calling to be the presence of Christ in their community.

Although obedience and follow-through can hardly be called innovations, they are frighteningly rare in our churches. Many, perhaps most, mission statements are hammered out with blood, sweat, and tears—only to collect literal or metaphorical dust once complete. But it is not a mission until it is implemented, no matter how eloquent the statement. Leonardtown has owned and embodied their mission. Having heard God's call for them, both pastors and laypeople have taken personal risks to be Christ's presence to their neighbors. Without obedient risk, mission always fails.

The fundamental lesson from the turnaround in Leonardtown is that mission always drives innovation. Innovation alone does not accomplish anything of kingdom significance. What matters most in the Leonardtown church is that innovation was not the primary agenda. Mission was the agenda, above all else, and innovation became a necessity if the church was going to fulfill its mission. When mission became the driving motivation, and when the leadership embraced the willingness to risk failure in pursuit of the mission God had given them, innovation became the obvious next step. Doing what they had always done would not fulfill the mission. Carefully considered innovation was the necessary means of fulfilling their reason for existence: being the presence of Christ in their community.

Learn More
- http://lcotn.com
- Gallup's Faith Member Engagement survey: http://www.gallup.com /products/174866/faith-member-engagement.aspx
- StrengthsFinder survey: https://www.gallupstrengthscenter.com

Discussion Questions

1. What parallels between your own setting and the Leonardtown setting might offer a fresh insight for your planning?

2. What do you think of Leonardtown reclaiming their traditional building as a key missional strategy? Is that an option for your church?

3. How do your people view the neighborhood nearest your local church setting? What contact do you already have with your nearest neighbors?

4. How can you turn the attention of your church from an inward, survival orientation to an outward, missional vision?

5. What low-hanging fruit do you see as you look around your church for means of making contact in the community? What are some easy ways to begin building relationships with folks outside your church?

6. What could your church do if the fear of failure was set aside?

7. What existing ministries or services are at work near your church that might be a place for partnership or cooperation?

8

The Church Where Failure Was Impossible

Name: Sunnyvale

Denomination: Church of the Nazarene

Location: Sunnyvale, California

Size: Small (20)

Ethnic Makeup: 60% Caucasian; 40% Other (Latin American, African American, Filipino, Hawaiian, Native American, Chinese)

"WE KNEW that we could try anything without fear of failure," says Jeff Purganan, pastor of Sunnyvale Church of the Nazarene. "We couldn't fail because this church should have closed long ago."

The Sunnyvale church started in 1955 in an old barn house on an orchard. They grew, bought land, and built a beautiful building with pews to seat 450. Like most Nazarene churches in Northern California, they experienced booms in the '70s, '80s, and '90s. But as demographics shifted and the culture changed, they didn't make the transition well. In

Northern California, most of the founding English-speaking congregations dwindled while new congregations in a dizzying array of languages popped up.

Sunnyvale kept afloat during hard times by sharing space with a vibrant, Spanish-speaking congregation, but everyone knew the English-speaking church was on life support. When Jeff and his wife, Meredith, arrived for the interview in 2010, only six stubbornly faithful church members were there to meet them. Faced with declining numbers, the church had deferred maintenance on their building so long that it was a tattered shell. The roof leaked; the basement seeped; there was mold in every room. Meredith says it rained in the pastor's office. To make matters worse, any major repairs would trigger municipal building-code requirements to make the entire structure earthquake proof and accessible to the disabled. The total remodel estimates came in around a cool million dollars.

Against all odds, within two years under Jeff's leadership, the church had grown to thirty regular attenders (leading the district with 500 percent growth!). They developed an initial plan to sell their old, oversized building and buy a smaller building more suited to their actual needs. They hoped to get something with multiple usage possibilities, ideally with space they could rent to a preschool.

The Crazy Idea That Changed Everything

But Pastor Jeff had a nagging thought: *What if we invest in people first and buildings later?* That question had roots in two conflicting realities. First, Sunnyvale, California, sits in the heart of Silicon Valley. Its residents are primarily young, highly educated, tech-driven immigrants. They come from diverse religious backgrounds, and they want to be part of organizations that are changing the world in vibrant and tangible ways. Only a very creative expression of church would be effective in this missional context. Sunnyvale Church of the Nazarene, on the other hand, was made up of mostly white retirees. They had already participated in church plants in their younger years, and they weren't really interested in innovating all over again. They just didn't have the physical or emotional energy it would take to start over in a new place, much less in new ways. Restarting with a traditional church model didn't make sense either, though, because there were already three other traditional Nazarene churches fewer than five miles away.

Finally, just as they were about to pull the trigger on the church restart, Jeff had a "come to Jesus" meeting with the church board. He told them, "We talk about the church being the people, yet the full investment of this restart is going to be in buildings. None of it is going to be in people or ministry. So what if we start with people instead of a building? Then, when the people need a building, we'll have the funds to do that." Instead of buying a new building, Sunnyvale Church decided to sell everything and hire a bunch of interns. With the district's approval, they sold their old building for $6.5 million to a residential developer, and they established an endowment to empower new forms of ministry. As Jeff explains, this was only possible because the faithful giving by decades of Sunnyvale church members "had accumulated as an asset in the form of our church property. At the sale of the property, that investment of time, service, and money became a deep financial resource."

This transition was unusual in other ways too. It just so happened that New Life Church of the Nazarene, just a few miles away in Cupertino, was in desperate need of a new pastor, new members, and new resources. The proceeds of the sale of the Sunnyvale building became an endowment managed by the district in the name of the Sunnyvale church, and the Sunnyvale members all transferred their membership to New Life. The Spanish-speaking church that had been renting from Sunnyvale moved to the New Life facility as well, giving New Life a significant financial boost. Instead of being a bivocational pastor of Sunnyvale and a photographer, Jeff became a bivocational pastor of New Life and the director of a new internship project.

This unique arrangement kept open the possibility of restarting Sunnyvale Church of the Nazarene later, without disentangling its financial resources from New Life Church. In 2013, Sunnyvale was listed as an inactive church. In 2015, it was listed as a district assignment. In 2017, Sunnyvale Church officially became a new church, parented by Cross-Roads Community Church of the Nazarene in nearby Palo Alto. This flexibility and mobility feel pretty normal to people living in the ever-changing heart of the tech industry.

The Possibility Project

Nestled in Silicon Valley, where you can throw a rock and hit three tech startups, an alternative approach to church planting makes sense. The Possibility Project emerged from three separate streams of thought:

1) missionary tent-making to engage secular work as part of a spiritual mission; 2) millennial culture's emphasis on community building; 3) the technology industry's emphasis on improving our world. The confluence of these three ideas was the Possibility Project's commitment to discipling young adults in intentional Christian community. They secured two apartments and recruited their first four interns in 2013. The purpose of the internship is to help these students learn to be disciples of Jesus while living in the real world.

Jeff explains that many young Christians struggle with the transition from the relatively sheltered world of youth groups and Christian universities to working out their faith in secular companies. Similarly, many churches struggle with welcoming home these young adults in meaningful ways. As Jeff sees it, part of the struggle is in the implicit limit of the church's invitations to young adults: "For example, if you're a recent college grad, the first thing the church asks you to do is children's ministry. You're an engineer or a programmer or something, with no kids and no experience teaching—but we ask you to do things completely outside your training and passion. The church needs a vision that rivals what you get in the tech community. If you're twenty-two and you work at Facebook or Google, they don't limit your access to baby projects—limited sets of small problems. Instead, they say, 'What are you best at? How can we maximize what you have to offer us?'"

Because the Church of the Nazarene firmly believes in early discipleship and invests heavily in our universities, we pour twenty-two years of resources into developing adventurous, intelligent adults who are ready to change the world. But, as Jeff explains, "we don't have any pipeline to help them come back and reinvest in our churches and communities." The Possibility Project is that pipeline for the Bay Area. Their intensive discipleship plan is a tapestry interweaving three distinct threads: education, internships, and formation.

The educational element is intense. The interns read one book a month for two years, meeting weekly to apply what they are studying. Topics range from relationships to finances to theology to church governance and just about everything in between—covering everything a young adult needs to develop a stable, holy, vibrant life. Next, since this is an internship program, part of the expectation is that each intern will get involved with a local church or ministry and help with events on the district. For example, several interns serve on staff at nearby churches, and all the interns help with the Northern California summer camps for children or youth. In addition, each intern is empowered and funded to initiate special projects in the church or community where they serve. These special projects have been an important catalyst in earning the district's trust.

First, each intern is tasked with giving their church a "first-impression rose." (This is a cultural allusion to *The Bachelor* and *The Bachelorette* TV series on ABC. Early in each season, one of the contestants is given a rose as a sign that the contestant has made a good first impression. The interns adapt the idea by doing something practical to make a good first impression with their new church.) They choose a small project that's relatively easy to fix: new paint for a nursery, a few microphones, a leaky toilet, and so on. Then they get approval for a grant of up to $500 from the Possibility Project, and they do the work and bless their new community right from the beginning. Jeff explains, "It's really hard to teach faithful churchmanship. But for the cost of $500 a year, we are helping interns embrace their role as change agents and understand that, for relatively small amounts, they can really improve their church. We hope that will continue with their own funds after they leave our program."

Second, the interns join in with one of their church's projects or partners. Possibility Project is a big believer in the critical importance of the "first follower" in forming a movement.[1] Sometimes, the most important act of leadership is joining in with something good that's already happening. So the interns look around at what their church is already doing or helping with, and then with another $500 grant, they join in to make it better. The idea is for the interns to develop habits of generosity and community support, and it seems to be working. Some of the interns are already pledging personal funds to organizations they first supported through a grant.

Third, the interns all have the opportunity to invest in something outside their church. Some interns support an existing organization like Cru (Campus Crusade for Christ) or Alpha Pregnancy Center. Others embrace the opportunity to try new ideas with a little funding and support. "As a twenty-something Christian," Jeff says, "there were lots of places I could go to participate in traditional, liturgical-Christian, church stuff, but there was nowhere I could go to try out a new idea or to experiment with something outside the traditional church structures." By providing this freedom to innovate, Possibility Project functions as the research and development department for their district.

So far, the most successful project to grow out of incubation phase is Saving Acts, started by intern Katie Delgado (who also works full-time at Facebook). The mission of Saving Acts is "to share stories of goodness from and for the global church."[2] Sometimes missionaries and pastors are so busy that they don't have time to tell their stories. Even when they do have the time, they may not be particularly skilled as artists or storytellers. Saving Acts connects missionaries and other frontline workers with photographers, journalists, and videographers. In 2016, Saving Acts joined with Nazarene Compassionate Ministries, Nazarene Youth International, and Extreme Nazarene to send creative artists to Sierra Leone, Sri Lanka, and Ecuador, and their work was featured prominently in two issues of *NCM Magazine*. Saving Acts also has a partnership with the Northern California district for the Church of the Nazarene to document and celebrate their partnership with Nazarene Seminary of the Americas (also known as SENDAS) in Costa Rica.

Saving Acts is assembling creative partners all over the world who are eager to use their artistic gifts in service to God's mission. "Beautiful and redemptive stories from God's people need to be told, and creative media professionals can dramatically increase the reach and production quality of these stories."[3] Young adults who are lost with a hammer but good with a camera have often felt left out of missions, but Saving Acts is paving the way for them to give their best for the best causes.

However, as important as the educational and practical elements are, according to the interns, the most important part of Possibility Project is its formational power. Over and over again, the interns express the critical value of having a safe space to explore their doubts about God and church and to experiment with new ways of being church. In the book *The Rise of the Nones*, James Emery White explains that the fastest-growing religious segment in America is the group of people with no official affiliation.[4] Faced with only two options—A) church as I've always known it, or B) no church at all—today's young adults are choosing option B more often than ever before. The Sunnyvale interns live in this milieu and share the same tendencies. The Possibility Project, however, gives them a venue to explore a new option: C) experiment with new modes of church.

Patrick Jenkins, who is now a youth pastor in Eureka, California, explains, "I didn't trust any churches. I didn't feel like I could trust being in a Christian community and still being myself. I felt kicked out of the church, but I didn't feel like God had kicked me out. My time out here was fantastic because it was very healing. There was a lot of growth in finally being able to be fully me and be fully accepted with all of my doubts and different language. I was able to discover what it means to be a Christian and not be like the predominant, southern-evangelical Christian."

Alicia McClintic, a current Possibility Project intern who also serves as the associate pastor at CrossRoads Community Church, expresses similar sentiments: "I had also been part of a community with a lot of cynical and disillusioned, millennial Christians. They were a group that was really interested in deconstructing Christianity. It took me a while to realize that I was done with my deconstructing and ready to rebuild. While I had been hurt by the church in several ways, I wasn't ready to give up on the church. This was a chance to try new things while still working with the church in more traditional formats."

One of the greatest strengths of the Possibility Project seems to be that it has given space for young adults, arguably the church's most neglected and vulnerable demographic, to reconnect with local churches in meaningful ways. Two dozen millennials have uprooted their lives, embraced a rigorous internship, and volunteered their time—all in the hope of fully embodying their Christian faith. And it's working beautifully.

But Still, Startup Struggles

Ask anyone in Silicon Valley, and they'll tell you—starting a new organization is tough. The highs are higher, and the lows are lower than working for an established business. It can be isolating and draining and confusing. Jeff and the interns have experienced all of this. For the first few years, Jeff felt like he was the only one who really got his vision, but part of that was that the vision was still blurry even for him. "Until recently, most people couldn't see what I thought I could see," Jeff adds. "It was like I was given a handful of seeds, but I didn't really know what they would produce. I just knew that these seeds would produce good fruit if we planted them, but I didn't know what kind of fruit or how long it would take."

Now Jeff understands that the district put a lot of faith and trust in him by empowering him to try something completely outside the box, but at first Jeff didn't feel any of that affirmation. Jeff laments, "All I ever heard was silence, questions, and criticism." In retrospect, he can see that the subcommittee supervising Sunnyvale must have been supportive because they gave him so much freedom, but they only asked questions based in traditional measurements like, *Why isn't your membership growing?* Jeff summarizes, "We didn't know how to speak the same language. I was talking in visionary terms, and they were talking in institutional terms. We just kept talking past each other."

But part of the struggle was also that it takes a long time for people to really understand a new model. Jake Duckworth, the lead pastor of Sunnyvale's parent-affiliated church (CrossRoads) explains this difficulty: "There was pretty serious pushback and skepticism from a lot of places at the onset. Three years just isn't long enough for most people on the district to really get it. Even my church, as close as they are to Possibility Project, they still don't really get it."

However, the district seems to be catching on to the impact (both current and potential) of Possibility Project. After a few years of working bivocationally, Pastor Jeff is earning a full-time salary as the director of Possibility Project. Even more encouraging, the district is beginning to think about duplicating this model in other locations. A few churches that have extra housing available are thinking of bringing in interns with guidance from the Sunnyvale crew. There is even talk of starting a second internship hub on the northern end of the Bay Area.

Another struggle for Possibility Project has been in the transience of their target group. Young adults are still figuring life out, and they are by nature a bit unstable. Several interns have left the program early to pursue romantic relationships or more formal education. Dealing with those transitions seems to be a necessary cost of internship programs.

A third key struggle was simply the ambiguity of working in a start-up. They were building the wagon while they were driving it. Several interns said this was the hardest part for them. Bailey explained, "With any new thing, even as there is lots of space, that can be frustrating and difficult. I didn't always know what we were doing, and the control side of me wanted to know exactly what the plan was."

Claudette, one of the early interns, mentioned the difficulty of explaining the program to other pastors on the district. "There wasn't really anything to come into. I remember in the first year, when we would set up meetings with pastors, no one knew who we were or what this was all about. That produced a lot of anxiety."

Patrick said, "Because we're still building the program, the vision is there, but it hasn't fully coagulated into what the program will actually become in time. That's Jeff's strength and weakness at the same time."

For Alicia, the openness was part of the struggle and the blessing. "Jeff helped me dream of what is possible just by asking me, 'What are you good at? What does it mean for you to be faithful with who you are?'" That made the whole process open-ended for her, giving her the freedom to discover herself as a person and as a minister, but it also put the responsibility of discovery squarely on her shoulders.

Still, for all the struggle of ambiguity in the beginning years, everyone involved affirms that they have settled into something beautiful and empowering. The interns, the churches, and the district all agree that those seeds that Jeff planted in 2013 are producing very good fruit.

Impact on the District

The Possibility Project has done significantly more than restart a church in a creative way. In addition to jumpstarting innovation for the whole Northern California district, they have three distinct, district-wide impact zones. The influx of energetic young adults has been a huge boost to the NorCal district's youth ministries. On an aging district, youth workers are hard to come by. Possibility Project has injected new energy, new ideas, and new vitality into nearly every district youth event. A few interns do their practicums as youth pastors, and Patrick has graduated out as a full-time youth pastor.

In addition, Possibility Project has become the human resources department for the district. Churches basically get the opportunity to engage in an extended interview process. The vast majority of their interns are still in the area, and several are in ministry roles in various churches on the district. Because of the magnetic pull of the Possibility Project, local churches have access to a much larger candidate pool when they are ready to hire.

One of the unexpected fruits of the extended internship and discipleship process is that it empowers women for ministry. Several women who had never felt truly qualified or equipped for ministry finally felt strengthened and emboldened to affirm and engage their callings. Claudette serves as a music pastor. Bailey is a volunteer music leader. Alicia is serving as an associate pastor while she continues seminary. Celia attends a Chinese-speaking seminary in the San Francisco area and is on staff at San Francisco New Life Church.

The biggest measurable impact for the district might be financial. Sunnyvale netted $6.5 million from the sale of their building, and that nest egg has grown to more than $8 million. Those funds are invested in two ways. Half is managed by a financial advisor investing in stocks and bonds, and the other half is used to finance or refinance loans for other churches on the district. In the Church of the Nazarene, most districts function as the guarantor for local church loans, but the money usually comes through banks or credit unions. With the Sunnyvale endowment, the NorCal district was able to finance about a dozen church mortgages or improvement loans at lower interest rates.

For some churches, this refinancing has been a game changer. In 2003, Livermore Church of the Nazarene purchased and renovated a large building with the capacity for 350 people. After reaching an average attendance of 175, the church faced a series of crises that led to almost a decade of decline. By 2012, they had shrunk to about 45 people, and the building felt like a financial albatross. For nearly a decade, they had only been able to pay the interest on their $1.7-million debt. Then their credit union informed them that their interest rate was going to go up from 6 percent to 8 percent. The church was desperate for an escape. The district, empowered by the Sunnyvale endowment, offered to refinance the loan at 5 percent, which enabled the church to avoid dumping their building at a below-market price. More importantly, according to Pastor Curtis Lillie, "We actually got to prayerfully discuss, over an extended period of time, whether this building would actually help us do the ministry we felt God had called us to do."

Freed from impending doom, Livermore started to view their building as an asset and got creative. At one point, they were renting their space to seven different churches. The district also loaned them additional funds to make improvements, which enabled them to rent out a portion of their building to a furniture store. That subdivided portion now produces enough annual income to pay their total base mortgage.

Curtis says the loans from the Sunnyvale endowment completely changed the ethos at Livermore. Previously, new ideas were immediately squashed with someone saying the church didn't have the money to do that. "It was a paralyzing thought process," Curtis summarizes, "that kept us from considering new possibilities." But after the loan and the building adaptations, the church is dreaming again. Once they pay back their improvement loan, they plan to invest more in both local and international missions.

Altogether, the district has provided loans to more than a dozen churches, saving those churches more than $2 million in interest pay-

Lessons for a District

The Northern California district for the Church of the Nazarene played a key role in empowering the innovation of Sunnyvale Church. They let a creative and unproven idea go forward even though they weren't sure how it would play out. They gave Jeff and the interns a great deal of freedom and eventually fully funded Jeff's salary out of endowment earnings. That trust shouldn't be underestimated. On the other hand, Jeff and the interns didn't feel a lot of explicit, verbal support from the district. Here are a few lessons church leaders, networks, and denominations can learn from the Sunnyvale experiment.

(1) Listen to all ideas, even the ones that sound crazy, and give the best ideas a chance even if the outcome is uncertain.

(2) Reconsider how to use proceeds from building sales. The standard practice is to invest the funds immediately in new church plants. However, consider what would help your organization innovate most.

(3) Be creative with structure and polity. The regulations exist to help the church, so flex the structure as necessary to help new expressions of church thrive.

(4) Communicate support intentionally and repeatedly. Innovation is hard and lonely work. Even if organizational leaders don't fully get what our young innovators are doing, we still need to go out of our way to offer encouragement and positive feedback.

(5) Find experienced innovators to support your young, creative leaders. Young pastors need mentors who will support them in the journey, without trying to control what they do. Business entrepreneurs may be able to add another helpful layer of mentoring.

ments over the next twenty-five years. But the effect extends well beyond the actual loans. Several other churches have used this endowment as leverage to refinance at lower rates with their original lenders, freeing more money for God's mission.

Future of Sunnyvale

So far more than twenty interns have worked with Possibility Project. Many of them still participate in the Sunday night potluck and worship services that happen at the men's house. For now, that is the main event of Sunnyvale Church of the Nazarene, but they have more plans and dreams. Ten percent of all tithes and offerings collected are committed to increasing the principal in their endowment so they can invest in even more interns in the future. Sunnyvale is also beginning to dream about new programs under the Possibility Project umbrella. One of their interns has dreams of converting open space in CrossRoads Community Church into a small-business incubator. Jeff and some friends are dreaming of forming an organization called Creative Castle as an internship program specifically for Christian artists.

Sunnyvale leaders are also taking an active role in district-wide strategic planning. In early 2017, the NorCal district approved a plan for Possibility Project to hire two staff members who will also work part-time for the district in youth and compassionate ministries. On the entire district of around one hundred congregations, there are only two paid youth workers. Nearly all of the district youth leaders are lead pastors with young children, so they can't make district functions a priority. These two new staff members will mentor volunteers and coordinate efforts in youth and compassionate ministries around the Bay Area. Jeff explains, "Since we have some money available and an open template, we can play and experiment with any ideas that might help solve things for the district."

What does the future look like for Sunnyvale Church of the Nazarene beyond the Possibility Project? The parent-affiliated model with Cross-Roads Church has been mutually enriching, so that partnership may continue indefinitely. They are also considering various other options, including a house church network. The possibilities are endless. The only guarantee seems to be that they will have more crazy ideas that change everything.

Find Out More
- https://www.thepossibilityprojectchurch.org
- http://www.savingacts.org
- To see some of the photos and journalism by Saving Acts, check out http://www.ncm.org/magazine.html. (See stories on Sierra Leone in Summer 2016 and stories on Sri Lanka in Winter 2016.)

Discussion Questions

1. Have you seen churches in your area in a similar situation to Sunnyvale when Jeff arrived (tiny congregation in an oversized, aging building)? What happened to those churches?

2. Jeff had a crazy idea that changed the whole course of Sunnyvale and possibly the Northern California district. What are some of the best crazy ideas you've had (or heard of)? What might happen if your church actually tried some of them?

3. Most churches in North America are struggling to reach millennials. What is Sunnyvale doing differently to help young people engage?

4. This story is full of ambiguity and the unknown. They still don't know for sure where they are headed. How does that make you feel? Could you see yourself or your church taking this kind of risk?

5. The Northern California district gave Sunnyvale a lot of freedom but perhaps not enough support. What can churches in your area do to cultivate an environment of innovation that extends beyond the bounds of one local church?

9

The Scum of the Earth Church

Name: Scum of the Earth Church

Denomination: Unaffiliated/Nondenominational

Location: Denver, Colorado

Size: Medium (150)

Ethnic Makeup: 80% Caucasian; 15% Latino; 5% Other

—⊷—

For it seems to me that God has put us apostles on display at the end of the procession, like those condemned to die in the arena. We have been made a spectacle to the whole universe, to angels as well as to human beings. We are fools for Christ, but you are so wise in Christ! We are weak, but you are strong! You are honored, we are dishonored! To this very hour we go hungry and thirsty, we are in rags, we are brutally treated, we are homeless. We work hard with our own hands. When we are cursed, we bless; when we are persecuted, we endure it; when we are slandered, we answer kindly. We have become the scum of the earth, the garbage of the world— right up to this moment.

—1 Corinthians 4:9–13

—⚊—

IN 1 CORINTHIANS, Paul has to defend his ministry because this church in Corinth, full of young and immature Christians, is confused. Paul has to explain the hows and whys of the work he did in Corinth. As this church experiences the surprising and paradoxical nature of kingdom life, confusion swirls around the roles of the leaders. The life of an apostle, according to Paul, is not glamorous, nor is it for the faint of heart. In fact, it is an undertaking that requires a huge amount of sacrifice. In one of his most colorful moments of prose, Paul describes their work as having "become the scum of the earth, the garbage of the world." No wonder the church today has struggled to send out apostles. Even if the church understands the role of the apostle and identifies those with said gifts, being the scum of the earth and the garbage of the world is hardly a job description many would willingly accept.

This difficulty makes the story of Scum of the Earth Church in Denver all the more beautiful. It is a story of the collision between the edge of the kingdom of God and the edge of society. It is at the same time both truly unlikely and exactly what you would expect from God. The apostle Paul says he and his coworkers only planted the seeds and watered them, but it was God who made them grow. This is a story of planting, watering, and watching God bring about a harvest of incredible beauty. There are many lessons to be learned from the birth and growth of Scum of the Earth Church, but it would be easy to confuse the uniqueness of their story with a blueprint for doing ministry in the margins.

Many have looked to Scum to glean techniques and models for imitation. If you show up to worship on a Sunday night in downtown Denver, you will find a gathering that is undoubtedly different from most churches. Out on the porch will be a group of inked, pierced, spiked, and otherwise ragged-seeming congregants, with a cloud of smoke marking their presence. Inside you will find a unique worship space pulsing with art in a variety of surprising forms. You'll know you've encountered something altogether different when you see the graffiti on the wall, paintings, drawings, handmade furniture, and bathroom walls covered in pennies and painted toilet seats. When the Communion server who offers you the body of Christ has more tattoos and piercings than an entire biker gang, you might do a double take just before a smile rises from your soul. All these things are unique and beautiful, but these are not the innovations that make Scum what it is.

You could come to visit Scum of the Earth Church, take notes on their unique space, note the way their people dress, mark the language that shapes their culture, and go away trying to imitate those things in order to be innovative yourself. This would entirely miss the point, however. Their key innovations are not a cool name, a Christian, ska-punk band, talented artists, or an edgy and exciting culture. All of those things are present, but they are not what have allowed Scum to experience breakthrough where so many others have failed. Instead, their story is one of authenticity, faith, trial and error, and a dogged commitment to love people in the margins.

Meet Mike

The story of Scum of the Earth Church begins with Mike Sares, the founding pastor. Mike is an unlikely person to be at the center of this story. He isn't a guy whom you would expect to pastor a church named Scum of the Earth. He doesn't have a mohawk, lots of piercings, or an indie, alt-rock band. He did, however, have a perfect kingdom résumé for this kind of undertaking. Mike ended up pastoring this church because he learned the hard way to listen to the voice of God and to respond to it. That is how apostolic work is born.

Growing up in a Greek Orthodox church, Mike's relationship with God was filled with many starts and stops. Even as he began to identify his calling to full-time ministry, he spent years alternating between a variety of jobs (a mill, a radio station, sales, etc.) while also serving in several roles with Young Life.[1] By the time he arrived in Denver, at age thirty-nine, with his family in tow, he had been waiting for fifteen years to fulfill his call to full-time ministry.

113

In the mid-'90s, Mike enrolled at Denver Seminary and worked part-time at Corona Presbyterian Church in downtown Denver. It was here, in a very traditional church, that Mike would begin to discover the people who would one day be part of the birth of Scum of the Earth Church. One Sunday at Corona, a few young adults showed up. They were an unexpected sight in this older-generation church. Mike discovered they were part of a local ska band. If you are wondering what exactly a ska band is, you aren't alone. Mike had no idea what ska music was. But he ventured out with a musician friend one night to hear this band play. (Ska is a blend of reggae and jazz that was birthed in Jamaica in the 1960s. It enjoyed a run of great success in the UK and U.S. in the 1990s and early 2000s. In its third wave, ska music featured a significant punk influence.)

Five Iron Frenzy, the band that had walked into Mike's church on that fateful Sunday, would eventually rise to have quite a following in Christian and secular music. Mike found an unexpected affinity for this group, and the friend who had joined his investigative outing ended up joining the band to play trombone. Mike became pastor, de facto manager, and mentor to Five Iron Frenzy. They integrated themselves into the church, and Mike helped them host a Bible study that became a gathering spot for twenty-somethings of all sorts.

When Losing Your Job Leads to a New Church

Following a leadership change, Mike's time at Corona came to an end, and he found himself in a familiar position: searching for the place that would finally fulfill his call to ministry. He was starting over—again. This forced change, however, would be the catalyst that changed everything. Several people close to Mike stepped up to offer support so he could plant a church with the seeds of this unique Bible study and young adult ministry. Mike took a gigantic leap of faith—something required in all apostolic work—and began to create something new.

Those who gathered with Mike to give birth to this new work brought with them all sorts of ideas about the type of church they wanted. A church where people didn't feel like they had to adapt to fit in. A church of genuine community. A church with financial transparency and integrity. A place for the arts, where beauty was created. They would eat together. They would have shared leadership. Men and women alike would lead, teach, and use their gifts. It would be the kind of place where the homeless could feel fully part of the community.

Leadership Insight: Look to Your Margins

Does your church have a pocket of people in the margins? Is there a Bible study or recovery group that reaches people most churches don't? Do you have a few families from a low-income area? Does an AA group meet in your building? Do you have a few people from one minority group? This group could be the growing edge for your church. How can you support this group with your hospitality? Maybe you get the families together for a meal and ask them about their friends. Maybe you host a cookout. Maybe some of them would be willing to host a Bible study in their homes. Maybe they have their own ideas about something that would be appealing or helpful to their neighbors. Start with the marginalized people you already have, and let them lead your whole church into the margins.

There was excitement within the team as they shared their ideas for what they could build together. One of the big questions was, "What do we call our church?" Reese Roper of Five Iron Frenzy suggested the name Scum of the Earth. He was pretty sure it was from the Bible somewhere, and he thought it would be a great name. Mike was not sold on it, though. Just imagine trying to raise support for a church called Scum of the Earth! But ultimately, the name stuck. More importantly, the heart of 1 Corinthians 4 was woven into the fabric of the community. From the beginning, it was a church where Christlike humility was present. This is how they would become good news for those who might otherwise not know the kingdom of God was open to them.

Since its founding in 2000, Scum of the Earth Church has experienced a remarkable journey, growing from a small, young adult Bible study into a thriving church community full of those they describe as the "right-brained and left out." As with all growth, however, there have been significantly challenging stages of development. A great name, a vision, an edgy band, and a willing servant are great resources for beginning a church, but much more is required to build something that will last.

Becoming Scum

Many visitors and church leaders who have visited Scum of the Earth over the years have been surprised that it is so much like other churches.

If you join them for worship, you will be treated to a music set, announcements, a sermon rooted in Scripture, prayers of the people, Communion, and a time of response. All of those things have a distinctly Scum flavor, but they are all present. They share a meal together every week after they worship. They have prayer groups, recovery groups, ministries to feed the hungry, retreats, mission trips, and hangout nights. Although these are all important for Scum, none of these activities is terribly unusual.

So what is it that has been so innovative about Scum of the Earth that has allowed it to minister to a people group that is almost entirely absent from most churches? The enduring wisdom from Scum's story finds its roots in 1 Corinthians 4, the passage that gave them their name. Scum has pioneered a new work as an outpost of the kingdom in the margins of our culture because it is a church where authenticity is far more than a tagline. Over the last twenty years, certain buzzwords have become nearly ubiquitous in the North American church: *relevant, community, authentic, sharing life together, missional, emerging*, etc. Scum doesn't care about buzzwords, though. In fact, one of their cultural standards is that they have an extremely low tolerance for BS (and people at Scum don't use the acronym). The fundamental innovation of Scum of the Earth Church—one that Mike and many of the other leaders had to learn the hard way—is true authenticity. The community of Scum works because people come as they are, often without the emotional energy to pretend to be someone else, and they find acceptance. Many churches want to minister to people on the street, young adults, and alternative subcultures, but they also want to retain their comfort. The wisdom of Scum is found in a place where the deep pain and sacrifice of authenticity are found.

Mike describes his journey to authenticity as a long process of learning to embrace his weaknesses instead of his strength. As Scum got off the ground, Mike found himself ministering to a culture that was completely foreign to him. He didn't grow up as part of a youth subculture; he was mainstream. Mike wasn't down and out because the system seemed bent against him; he thrived within the normal systems. Mike had a mortgage, a family, a long job history, and no addictions. To lead a church of young adults who belonged to another culture, he had to learn—like the apostle Paul—to become something else. This didn't happen by putting on a new style of clothes or imitating a certain look. It happened by learning to drop the façade of success and victory that often marks our church cultures. Mike had to find and embrace the common threads of brokenness that work their way across all of humanity. It is there—in the dark places of ourselves that we are afraid to show others —where authenticity and relevance truly begin.

Scum learned to embed authenticity into their church culture. One key has been developing a high tolerance for ambiguity. This is not a lack of clarity in theology or purpose but, rather, an acceptable tension rooted in the ambiguity of how their people live. The people of Scum are all in different places with their lifestyles, addictions, sexuality, and morality. Can you keep the main thing the main thing while being comfortable with ambiguity? Most churches cannot live within this tension. The pressure to make people conform is strong for most of us. This is where faith turns into religion. We want to present a church where there are certainty and victory, and we end up in a place far from authenticity. Acceptance without approval is a key part of Scum being Scum.

So, if acceptance is practiced, it must also be preached. The sermon itself must become a signifier of this level of acceptance. The preacher can't merely tell others to practice acceptance and transparency; the preacher must live this out. Mike realized that, when he preached, he had to demonstrate that even the pulpit was a place of acceptance. This required Mike not to celebrate his victories but to bare his scars and share his struggles. Without displaying his own brokenness, Mike could never lead others to a place of healing.

The pulpit also had to become a place of diversity. Early on, Mike realized he had to put younger leaders up front as often as possible. As an outsider, he needed indigenous leaders, from the Denver streets and punk culture, to be focal points of the community. They made difficult choices about who fit that vision and need. Sometimes it meant turning aside gifted leaders, who wanted to be part of Scum, because their involvement would have ultimately blocked the path of younger leaders who better represented the culture. If the corporate worship service can be a place of authenticity and acceptance, then hurting and lost people might actually believe this can be their home.

Of course, creating a worship service with such a high level of acceptance leads to all sorts of other challenges. How drunk or high is too drunk or too high to still participate in worship? Not many churches have to deal with that question! Mike tells the story of one service where this tension came to a head. Before and after the service, a group of people always hang out on the porch in a haze of smoke. This is actually a key place of hospitality and ministry. On this particular night, Mike was hanging out on the porch as a greeter and bouncer (the latter not being a role most churches need). He let a slightly drunk guy into the service, but as the service went on, the guy became more and more drunk as the alcohol metabolized in his bloodstream. As the band played, the guy began to shout out between each song, "Turn around, turn around!"

Eventually, Mike (the bouncer/pastor/greeter) had to remove him from the service. Mike asked him, "What are you doing? Why are you being disrespectful?" The guy got angry and began to shout profanities at Mike and then finally left.

Then he came back twenty minutes later, apologized, and asked why Mike had kicked him out. "Didn't the band know the song 'Turn Around'? It plays on Christian radio all the time!" Mike finally realized this guy had just been shouting out a song request for the band—which is a pretty normal behavior at any concert.

Another common encounter Mike had was with a young man who was part of the Goth culture. He came to church for the first time totally decked out in black eyeliner, black nail polish, fishnet stockings, a skirt, and black boots. Mike says he was trying to get a reaction. Mike made sure to interact with him in a way that showed that the wrapping didn't matter.

One thing Mike has learned is that people will often present the most radical form of themselves to test your acceptance. That guy ended up sticking around and becoming part of their community. Other folks who have shown up in similar garb have ended up on the church staff.

When Scum Grows Up

As it has grown and matured, Scum of the Earth Church has confronted difficult choices and learned hard lessons that are common to most churches. The default direction of a church is always to grow inward, to take care of your own people, to raise your children, and to look inside your doors. Inertia moves inward. Mike has such a pastor's heart that he wants to keep all the sheep in the flock and to take care of their needs. But at Scum, valuing the togetherness of the people ended up distracting them from their mission.

Scum always met at 6:30 on Sunday nights, which is way later than most churches. But it fit their demographic. As people got older, got real jobs, and had kids, that 6:30 p.m. time slot grew more difficult. So they started a Sunday morning service with a liturgical style. Mike believed it would be great as a connection point for a whole different group of people. The leaders of Scum saw this service as a first step in becoming a community of variety.

Scum ran this morning liturgical worship service for eight years, and ultimately it had a significant impact in both expected and unexpected ways. A whole different community formed around this Sunday morning service, but it lacked the missional zeal that the church valued. Overall, the church became increasingly inwardly focused. Men's ministry, women's ministry, and children's ministry all grew to serve this new community. On one hand, it all seemed like great progress. In reality, however, the church began to see fewer and fewer conversions and baptisms. The inward pull of serving themselves caused them to lose their missional focus. They were no longer a missional outpost at the edge of God's kingdom.

As a team of leaders, they finally came to the decision that they would reunite the services at the new time of 5:00 p.m. in an attempt to recapture who they were. They didn't want to do a Sunday morning service because there are plenty of Sunday morning churches. The earlier evening time slot was friendlier to families and working folks, and it allowed Sunday morning to become a space for mission. However, combining the services and refocusing on mission led to significant fallout. Taking away the morning service cost them some of the best and brightest leaders they had. People who had grown out of their edginess began to leave because they no longer felt part of Scum's mission.

The mid-course correction was extremely painful. Being pruned is awful. No church wants to lose valued members of their community. For a church built on radical acceptance, it is particularly painful to be rejected by those you love even as you try to build a place of acceptance. Even so, protecting their mission of accepting those whom society rejects has proven to be the most important part of Scum's identity. And they have had to fight over and over again to maintain this outward-leaning identity of acceptance.

When Scum Multiplies

Over the years, Scum of the Earth Church has had the privilege of helping leaders in other parts of the country start their own outposts of the kingdom. They have officially launched two new churches, one in Colorado Springs and one in Seattle. Here the joys and pains of pioneering work were clear. Both churches met with great breakthroughs and significant struggles. However, neither one was able to survive the leadership transition after the founding pastors left. One church closed their doors after three years, and the other lasted eleven years.

In the world of innovation and pioneering, these are vitally important efforts. Some might look at those new churches and tell their story by saying that, ultimately, they didn't succeed. Yet taking new territory is such hard work that undoubtedly the ending of those efforts doesn't remotely tell the story of their success. Leaders, shaped and formed by the pioneering culture of Scum, were able to go out and plant seeds that grew in difficult soil. Those seeds have spread and sown other seeds, the harvest of which may never be fully known. But innovation requires a willingness to risk and to sacrifice even if you don't see the harvest yourself.

Scum learned vital lessons in replicating their culture and training leaders through the church-planting process. The life and death of those communities was determined by their leadership and by their inability to raise up and shape new leaders. Long-term innovation and pioneering is just as reliant on having leaders who follow up and expand the work of apostles as it is on having these pioneering leaders who go and take new territory. Leaders must reproduce themselves in other leaders for the fruit of their labor to continue beyond their direct influence and tenure. The struggle of those new communities was ultimately in their lack of ability to produce the next generation of leaders necessary to sustain long-term vitality.

However, Scum continues to invest in the process of replicating leaders with Scum DNA. For years, Mike Sares has been grooming his replacement. Jesse Heilmann, who is a more natural fit for the alternative culture of Scum, is now co-lead pastor with Mike. Scum's future, and its culture, will be entrusted into his hands. Scum also continues to help new leaders plant churches with their particular cultures. In late 2016, Scum helped plant a new community in Scotland. Scum has gone international! Through their successes and failures, they have continued to pioneer new works of the kingdom.

True authenticity is hard and dirty work. You can't stay clean and comfortable if you are to become the scum of the earth, the garbage of the world. But Scum's ability to create a culture of true acceptance is at the core of their longevity. Maintaining vibrant, vigilant acceptance will be at the core of their future. Scum's story is worthy of so much praise and gratitude. They have tapped into a timeless and essential truth of the kingdom. Our churches' ability to become outposts on the edge of the kingdom of God is dependent on our ability to develop an authenticity that runs counter to our prevailing culture. The kingdom flourishes where people of all different walks come together to embrace each other, strip away the pretense of who they think they should be, and engage in the pursuit of God as they really are. That is the beautiful, unexpected, painful, joyful journey of Scum of the Earth Church.

Learn More

- http://www.scumoftheearth.net
- http://www.mikesares.com
- Check out the extensive "Scum of the Earth Church" page on Wikipedia.

Recommended Resources

- *Pure Scum: The Left-Out, the Right-Brained, and the Grace of God*, by Mike Sares (2011)

Discussion Questions

1. Scum of the Earth Church must have one of the most creative and poignant names in the history of all church names. What does the name of your church say about your congregation? How much does the name matter?

2. Scum of the Earth Church started because an unusual band invited a pastor to do a Bible study with their unusual friends. Are there any people in your church who might connect you to a unique subculture in your community?

3. Scum is full of Christians who don't fit our cultural expectations of what Christians "should" look like. What does that say about them, about us, and about church?

4. Pastor Mike had to learn to preach from his weaknesses rather than his strength. What are the implications of that for preaching and personal evangelism in your context?

5. As Scum works to live out radical acceptance, they know they will have to deal with ambiguity. What does it mean to truly accept someone into our churches without approving of everything they do? How can we show evidence of our acceptance of those whom others reject?

6. As they planted new churches, Scum discovered how difficult it is to replicate culture and pass innovation to future generations. Why is the transition from the second generation to the third generation of leaders so difficult? How can we overcome that difficulty?

10

The Church That Reclaimed Simplicity and Community

Name: Refuge

Denomination: Church of the Nazarene

Location: Durham, North Carolina

Size: Small (40)

Ethnic Makeup: 90% Caucasian; 10% Other

IN THE FACE of the dying North American church, many believe church planting is *the* answer. Just as the doors to one dilapidated building close for the final time, a sign pops up the on the side of the road, advertising a new church start.

Church plants *are* important, valuable, and necessary. We need people who stop clinging to what is dead to join in the new thing God is doing for the particular time and place to which we are called. There are trainings on how to plant churches and do it well, offering steps to spread the word, make a plan, gain critical mass, and move into a space. But Refuge Church did the opposite. No one was trained, and little planning happened. Refuge was a church planted on accident.

The first Refuge gathering started because of a conversation over lunch at Panera. Todd Maberry, an ordained elder in the Church of the Nazarene who worked at a nearby university, met with his friends Les and Chris in the summer of 2007. The three had previously attended church together, but more than a year had passed since they'd all left that congregation feeling hurt and discouraged. None of the three had planted roots in other congregations since that departure. They longed to experience deep Christian community once again. They craved space to be together, struggle together, and serve together.

And they decided to do something about it.

They sketched out a brief description of what they imagined would be what they called a missional small group, organized around the basic principle of love for God and others. Todd created an email address for the group. They collaborated on a list of folks to invite and shared an invitation to the first meeting via email, along with a simple document explaining what Refuge was, who it was for, where they would meet, and a plan for children.

On Sunday evening, September 7, 2007, those interested met for the first time in someone's home. The following Sunday evening, they gathered again, this time in someone else's home. The pattern continued, week after week, moving from house to house. Every week, an email went out giving details for the upcoming Sunday gathering. And every Sunday, people kept coming back. As they shuffled along that first year, conversations arose along the lines of identity. They spent many weeks discussing questions like "Who are we? What should the church be like?"

In January 2009, Todd asked people to come prepared with a written answer to those questions. This missional small group was still hesitant to call itself what it already was: a church. What else would you call a group gathered together each week sharing a meal, opening the Word, praying, sharing Christ's peace, and receiving Eucharist? The people of Refuge had accidentally become a church long before they were ready to admit it.

By the middle of 2009, almost two years into regularly meeting together, many of those who had been part of the original group had moved to other churches or away from the area. But Refuge was far from fizzling out. New people kept coming. Many were people who had no connection to the church where Todd, Chris, and Les had become friends many years earlier. These new faces saw Refuge as their church. So Todd stepped fully into the role of pastor, though he continued to serve bivocationally, taking no salary from the congregation. Todd polled the congregation for sermon series ideas and suggestions for scriptures to study and topics to discuss. He shared some of the teaching and facilitating responsibilities, utilizing Chris and Les in addition to nearby seminary students from Duke. Others volunteered to teach the children, arrange the hosting schedule, offer their homes for worship, bring food to the weekly meal, organize service opportunities, and manage finances. Refuge was notorious for making all decisions related to identity, form, worship, and service as a group. This kind of commitment requires immense patience. Often, group discussions took the place of preaching the Word as the church worked toward defining itself.

One identity marker that quickly rose to the surface without much debate was the descriptor *home church*. It doesn't take long to fall in love with this way of doing church. The most obvious benefit is cost. Meeting in different homes frees up the church budget. Imagine a budget without line items for rent, mortgage, maintenance, utilities, or grounds care. Meeting in private houses is also a way of lessening the environmental impact of a traditional church building. Churches often sit mostly empty from Monday to Saturday, using energy resources all week and then being reheated or cooled to prepare for Sunday worship. When meeting in members' homes, not only does the church conserve financial resources that can be funneled out into their community, but the congregation also resists the culture of consumption.

However, beyond the financial incentives, Refuge discovered that meeting in homes was also significant for becoming the type of church they envisioned. As new people began to join the church, folks who didn't previously know each other, the relational advantages became more obvious, even surpassing that of the cost benefit. Refuge wanted to be a church for those who wouldn't be comfortable in a traditional church. They wanted to be a community filled with people who had abandoned the church or felt abandoned by the church. Many people do not feel comfortable in traditional churches—and often for good reasons. Some have experienced deep hurt or very clear messages of unwelcome. However, some of those who won't enter a church building are willing to come over for dinner and a discussion on Sunday night. They also learned that going to church in someone's house shortens the distance that normally separates us from one another. Once you have been in someone's home, you know where they live, how they spend their money, and what their values are. In traditional church contexts, it can take weeks, months, even years to be invited into the home of another member. At Refuge, that distance is eliminated every single week.

Members began to notice that not only is the physical distance lessened, but meeting in homes also establishes a sense of vulnerability between the host and the guests. Imagine that you are hosting and one of your dishes is broken. That's a risk you took by inviting people over in the first place. Better to have people to share your space and belongings with than to hoard them only for yourself. It's also vulnerable for the guests. What if you or your kids break the host's dish? Will you be welcome again? While it may seem like a petty example, members found that this kind of spatial vulnerability and risk prepared them for vulnerability in other areas, such as sharing emotional struggles or life concerns.

Refuge has learned that the vulnerability of meeting in homes cannot be understated. You cannot slip in and out without being noticed. For a visitor, that first knock on the door is the hardest. Unless the visitor knows the host that particular week, visitors are often knocking on the door of a complete stranger's house and inviting themselves in for dinner. While that vulnerability can be challenging at first, it's also a gift that ensures that every person, whether visiting for the first time or coming back for the fiftieth, is known.

The Power Dynamic of Meeting in Homes

The biggest challenge of meeting in homes is the power dynamic between who can host church and who cannot host church, mostly due to space constraints. It's hard to fit thirty people into most living rooms. Refuge responds to this dynamic in at least four concrete ways:

1. *Tell the truth about it.* The dynamic loses some of its power when it is named aloud. It is most powerful when some people are unaware that it exists while others are painfully aware. Also, making everyone cognizant of the dynamic increases thoughtfulness in conversations about planning and hosting.

2. *Value the sharing of hospitality beyond hosting.* Many talk of hospitality as a gift of the Spirit, but the focus is often on the one who gives the

hospitality, not on the one who receives it. At Refuge, everyone gives and receives hospitality. A person unable to host church may bring a side dish to the weekly meal or stay after to help with the dishes. Another, unable either to host or bring food to share, still brings the gift of presence, by which all are changed because of their friendship.

3. *Visit the homes of some of the most marginalized: those in prison.* Four times a year, Refuge worships at Butner Federal Prison Complex, about twenty minutes from central Durham. On the weeks that Refuge worships at the prison, there is no additional service. The inmates host church those Sundays. Refuge goes to the same facility every quarter, where the population remains mostly constant over time. People get to know one another and look forward to seeing each other every three months.

4. *Meet in the park.* In the warmer months, Refuge meets for church in the park at least once a month. The park provides a neutralizing space, since no one person or family is hosting the whole group. Members simply bring their own picnic dinners and share the space together.

Innovation through Pastoral Transition

By 2011, Todd had begun to sense that it was time to move on, both for himself and for Refuge. He expressed his sense that Refuge was ready for a big step but that he didn't think he was the one to make that move. Todd began to discern that the person God was calling to be the next pastor was one of their own members, Megan Pardue, who would soon be graduating from seminary at Duke. When Todd explained his discernment process to Megan, she was surprised. After some consideration, she declined the suggestion. She was reluctant to commit to staying in the area after school, wanting to be flexible so her husband could take his turn in school. Todd didn't push too hard. He gave Megan some space to imagine herself in that role, and he took time to reflect with her about how the transition might look and what might need to change at Refuge before Megan could move into the role Todd would be vacating.

By the following summer, Megan had graduated from seminary and hadn't yet found a job. Her husband was accepted to school in the Durham area in the same week that Todd got a call to go to another church. That made things clear for Megan: she would be staying at Refuge, and Todd would be leaving. Megan and Todd began to pray together and work on a process to guide the congregation into the transition. Todd led the way, painting a vision of Refuge with a paid pastor, someone to take the reins and invest in the church and the community in ways he hadn't been able to do with so few hours to give to the church. In a unanimous vote, the congregation called Megan to be their pastor and to make the transition to paying a part-time pastoral salary. In December 2012, Refuge laid hands on Megan and commissioned her as their new pastor.

Bringing Megan on board marked an organizational shift for Refuge. While the egalitarian nature of the group is still a core value, there is now an official leader to make decisions so the group isn't required to do the long work of talking through every choice. When Megan became pastor, Refuge established a church board to offer support and to share the decision-making that was once delegated to the entire group. A church member created a website, whereas previously meeting times and locations were shared solely through email and word of mouth. Having a paid pastor moved Refuge into a more organized church structure, where it could flourish in new ways, while still maintaining the simplicity, informality, and community of meeting in homes for worship.

Experimenting toward Missional Living

It took Refuge a few years to gain their footing as the missional people they hoped to be. While always missional and outward with the tithes and offerings that came in, people desired other opportunities to serve and engage the larger community. This was a process of trial and error, experimenting with several different organizations and projects and discerning along the way.

Very early on, Refuge joined a faith team with a local nonprofit called Religious Coalition for Nonviolent Durham. In the Faith Team program, a group comprised of five to ten church members commits to walking alongside an individual (the Faith Team partner) who has been incarcerated or part of the criminal justice system.

Refuge was partnered with a teenager who had been in trouble with the law. The relationship between the faith team and this young woman had incredible glimpses of the kingdom, from throwing this pregnant teen mother a baby shower to repairing her grandmother's roof. One member even stayed up with her during her labor and the birth of her child. Abruptly, however, Refuge's teen partner cut off communication with the team. Many were deeply hurt that she no longer desired the relationship with the faith team, and other members mourned their unmet expectations. It took a couple of years before Refuge was ready to pursue something with such deep relational vulnerability again.

Instead, they moved into a series of one-time service projects. Refuge volunteered at the interfaith food shuttle, helped folks who were displaced with a city housing issue move into new housing, stained the deck and cleaned the house of a family with a chronically ill child, attended vigils for murder victims, and purchased and delivered Christmas gifts for low-income families.

In 2010, the idea arose for a community garden in an empty lot two houses down from Todd's house, in a low-income neighborhood. An enormous amount of energy went into creating the garden. The space had to be cleared, materials collected, garden beds built, seeds planted, watered, landscaped, weeded—all of the work that goes into gardening on land that was not yet ready to be tilled. Unfortunately, the lead volunteer —who had the most energy and passion for making the garden project happen—moved away during the first summer. Refuge had garden work days, met for Easter service in the garden, and tried to keep it going. Two more summers went by with them experimenting with different leadership ideas, watering schedules, and work days. But they finally admitted it was time to let the garden go. Thankfully, a local nonprofit, along with the neighborhood association, took over leadership of the garden with gusto. It still bears fruit for the community where Refuge planted it in 2010.

Then the church engaged in prayerful discernment about how they could best serve others and reach out. They asked questions like "How has God uniquely gifted our community? What are our strengths? What are we best at?" The answer that kept coming up was relationships. Because of their size and communal setting in homes, Refuge is uniquely relational and gifted in being with people. Relationships became the measuring rod for service engagement. The new evaluative questions became: "Does this partnership depend on long-term relational investment? Does it best utilize the relational strengths of our church?" If so, that partnership was worth pursuing.

Over the past four years, Refuge has engaged in service in three primary ways. First, as already mentioned, Refuge visits a prison for worship on a quarterly schedule, establishing and maintaining relationships with incarcerated men who are mostly forgotten by the rest of society.

Second, Refuge participates in a Circles of Support program run through a local nonprofit called Families Moving Forward. This partner-

> **Recommended Resource**
>
> As Refuge discerned how best to engage in service, the congregation read a book called *Living without Enemies: Being Present in the Midst of Violence*, by Samuel Wells and Marcia Owen.[1] The authors outline four approaches for social engagement: being for, working for, working with, being with. This quadrant of approaches provided Refuge with a framework to analyze their own strengths and weaknesses and to determine what types of partnerships would best utilize their gifts. As a deeply relational church, Refuge learned that their most natural approaches are *working with* and *being with* the community.

ship is similar to the faith team Refuge had previously, but the program is facilitated by a different local organization. A Circle of Support (four to ten members) commits to supporting a formerly homeless household for one year after they have transitioned out of homelessness and into housing. The circle offers relational support as challenges arise related to employment, housing, basic needs, family struggles, and other obstacles.

Third, Refuge supports one another. These acts of service occur on a week-to-week basis as various needs come up for different members. For at least two families with significant health issues and small children, supporting them has required serious time commitments, sharing of resources, providing childcare, visiting the hospital, bringing food, and even being advocates in the healthcare system. In these moments, the kingdom breaks through as Refuge lives into their mission: "to share the peace and community of God's abundant table."

Reclaiming Simplicity in Worship

When we think about worship innovation, we often think of churches with exceptionally skilled musicians, gifted artists, and master communicators who produce a high-caliber experience. But often, true innovation is rooted in making things simpler, not more complex. Innovation can be found in the everyday as much as in the extraordinary.

Every Sunday, Refuge's liturgy begins with the same call to worship. Though it's not words read aloud, it's no less of an invitation. Someone knocks at the door, and someone else opens it: "Hey! How are you? Come in."

Heavy arms and shoulders—laden with small children, potluck dishes, bags of items borrowed from friends, and a week's worth of burdens —all find relief in answering this call to worship and the response: "Yes, I'm here. I made it."

Everyone is invited immediately to the table, not yet for bread and wine, but for tacos, baked potatoes, lasagna, chili, or whatever the host may be serving. During dinner, people reconnect, deepening relationships from week to week. Following dinner, they gather in the living room to continue in worship, marking the start of the structured time together in the same place, instead of scattered about the house eating, playing, and talking. But this isn't the start of worship. Megan carefully avoids phrases like, "Let's get started," since the call to worship happened forty-five minutes earlier when people came in the door and came to the table. So, as the people gather together, young and old, worship *continues*.

Everyone is invited to participate in leading worship. The different parts of the liturgy are printed and put on clipboards. Volunteers pick up the clipboards from the stack, and if any clipboards lie unclaimed, one of the children passes them out to random adults of their choosing. First, one of the children reads a psalm reworded for young readers from *Psalms for Young Children*.[2] Next, they sing a song or two of praise, either *a cappella* or led with a guitar.

After singing, the people pray the same two prayers every Sunday: the prayer for Dana and the Refuge Common Prayer. The prayer for Dana is a responsive prayer asking God to be close to one church member who is serving as a missionary in Nigeria. The church takes their commitment to Dana so seriously that they pray for her every Sunday during worship. The prayer uses the familiar responsive line, "God, in your mercy," and all respond in unison, "Hear our prayer for Dana." The other weekly prayer is the Refuge Common Prayer. This is a prayer they wrote together in small groups in 2011, expressing what they profess to God about God, what they ask of God, and what values they hold together. This prayer functions for the community as a way to bring Refuge together in prayer before the Lord, to remind them of what they have done and left undone,[3] and to reaffirm who God is calling Refuge to be as a church.

On most Sundays, at this point, the children leave with an adult teacher and helpers to go outside or into another part of the house for their own lesson and playtime. Then the Word is preached, leaning on the community for participation. Preaching at Refuge lends itself to conversation, partially due to the nature of shared space. Imagine if you were in someone's living room and the pastor stood up to preach. With everyone else sitting around on sofas, kitchen chairs, or on the floor, it would feel a little awkward and unnatural. Instead, at Refuge, they sit in a circle, and the preacher sits at eye level with everyone else. But space isn't the only reason Refuge engages the sermon as a dialogue. Conversational preaching fundamentally makes space for doubts and questions. The sermons welcome interruptions. This method helps Refuge be church for people at different points in their faith journey, since they invite people to struggle with the sermon in real time. Conversational preaching also builds community because the congregation learns people's stories as they respond to the different questions Megan brings to the floor. Finally, this shared proclamation makes space for testimony. When some don't believe, the faith of others can support everyone, like the father who cried out to Jesus in Mark 9:24, "I do believe; help me overcome my unbelief!"

However, learning to practice conversational preaching was fraught with trial and error. When Megan first became the pastor of Refuge, she was at a loss for how to engage people in dialogue about Scripture. At first, Megan primarily preached for a bit and then asked, "What do you think?" This question elicited responses easily. The way the question is asked makes space for pushback, for the listener to agree or disagree. In fact, the question even allows for the listener to give the preacher a chance to clarify what has been said in the sermon up to this point. Week after week, Megan practiced asking some variation of that question, perhaps placing it at different points in the sermon or changing the wording slightly, to say something like, "Does anyone want to respond?"

Over time, though, she noticed that only a few people were answering the question and, usually, the same people each week. She also noticed that when some people responded, they felt as if they had to qualify their answer first with a comment like, "Well, I don't know much about . . ." or, "I'm not theologically trained . . ." Eventually, Megan realized she had been failing to ask good questions. Even worse, some felt marginalized by the question, as if their voice or response didn't matter as much as someone else's. Where some felt free to answer, others felt that, because they didn't consider themselves to be good thinkers, they had nothing to contribute. Further, *What do you think?* is not a compelling question; it doesn't move the participant toward God or toward others.

Slowly, Megan learned to ask better questions that would touch more than just a person's intellectual abilities. Christians are called to make disciples who follow Jesus with their whole bodies, so her questions needed to point in that direction. She began to vet her own questions through a rigorous lens:

- Does the question I'm asking engage the whole person?
- Does it engage any of their other senses?
- Does the question invite the congregation to draw on their experiences with God and the world?
- Could we frame this question by asking people to tell a story or share an experience?

As her questions improved, the dialogue improved. More people were willing to participate in the conversation, which helped the community become more and more connected with the Word and with each other.

Following the sermon, the children return to join with the adults in the ancient Christian practice of passing the peace. The pastor begins by saying, "The peace of the Lord be with you."

The congregation responds, "And also with you."

The pastor continues, "Let us show signs of peace to one another."

Then people greet each other with handshakes and hugs, saying to each other, "Peace of Christ" or, "Peace be with you."

The Refuge Common Prayer

God, you are the giver of life,
full of compassion, justice, and wisdom;
the Creator of every good thing.
Right now we pause to thank you for the blessings in our lives,
and to remember those who need a blessing.
(moment of silence)
May we be formed together by one another
so that your dreams become our dreams.
Make us into the type of community where all,
especially our children, are welcomed, nurtured, and known.
Do not allow us to become comfortable.
Rather, give us the ears to hear the cries of the oppressed,
the eyes to see the needs of the poor,
and the voices to speak with the marginalized.
Amen

The practice of passing the peace reminds followers of Christ that we are people of peace who are committed to peacemaking. It's not our own peace we share; it is Christ's peace.

Finally, people come to the table for the second time for the Lord's Supper, bookending worship at this most holy place once more. The Words of Institution are offered. Different people assist the pastor presiding with serving. Most of the children rush to the front of the line, forming an eager semicircle around the servers. They can barely make it through the Lord's Prayer. And they all know what to do. When Megan offers her one-year-old daughter a snack she's been waiting for, she immediately puts it into her mouth. But when she hands her a piece of the body of Christ, she holds it and waits for the cup. After Communion, Refuge closes with a simple sending word, a blessing or benediction until the work of the people continues again next week, when they will gather around a different table in a different home.

Imagining the Future in Homes

People often ask, "What happens when you grow too big?"

Others, assuming Refuge plans to follow a typical church-plant trajectory, ask, "How many more people do you need before you can move into a building?"

Still others say, with good intentions, "I'll be praying that God will give you what you need to get into a building."

However, after nearly a decade, Refuge remains deeply committed to meeting in homes. If the church family is too many to fit into one home, it will fit into two. If it's too many to fit into two, it will fit into three homes, and so on. In this way, Refuge may continue to innovate by becoming a network of house churches. The gifts of meeting in homes far outweigh the challenges. It's so central to who God has created Refuge to be that they cannot imagine another way.

Learn More

- http://www.refugehomechurch.org
- Interview with Pastor Megan on *This Nazarene Life*, produced by Brit Bolerjack; Season 1, Episode 9, http://thisnazlife.com/2016/08/08 /ep-9-rev-megan-pardue/
- "Talking about Conversational Preaching," *Holiness Today*, January /February 2017, http://holinesstoday.org/?q=talking-about-conversa tional-preaching-megan-m-pardue

Recommended Resources

- *Living without Enemies: Being Present in the Midst of Violence,* by Samuel Wells and Marcia Owen (2011)
- *The New Jim Crow: Mass Incarceration in an Age of Color Blindness*, by Michelle Alexander (2010)
- *The Word Before the Powers: An Ethic of Preaching*, by Charles L. Campbell (2002)

Discussion Questions

1. Does your congregation meet in a flexible space? Have you considered meeting in the round or outside in the summer?

2. Is your pastor willing to experiment with conversational preaching? Is your congregation willing to participate?

3. What are the unique ways God has gifted your congregation to love your neighbors? Do the areas of service where you're currently engaged match up with your unique gifts and resources?

4. If you are a small congregation or struggling to pay your bills, have you considered the benefits of meeting in homes? Is this a possibility in your context?

5. What would a common prayer in your congregation include? How might including a common prayer in weekly worship help to shape the mission of your church?

6. Is there a jail or prison near your church? Is your name on the visitor's log?

11

The Church Birthed as Missionaries

Name: Eden Community

Denomination: Church of the Nazarene

Location: Portland, Oregon

Size: Small (70)

Ethnic Makeup: 93% Caucasian; 7% Other (Hispanic, Asian)

THE STORY of Eden Community begins not with Eden itself but with a traditional congregation that imagined something new. In 2010, Pastor Mark Goodwin was serving as the senior pastor of Portland First Church of the Nazarene, a multi-staff congregation averaging 360 in Sunday worship on the west side of Portland, Oregon. Mark remembers many hours sitting around the table at board meetings, bemoaning the fact that their congregation was not reaching young adults. Despite the strong desire to minister to this demographic and attempts at doing so, they reached the conclusion that they probably were not going to be able to do it using the methods and approaches to ministry they already had in place. The disconnect was far deeper than a simple style issue, so addressing the problem with a change in music or a new program was not going to suffice.

God stirred in Mark a passion for ministering to young adults. He felt strongly and expressed to the board, "Time is not on our side. We can't wait. What's at stake is too great." He and the board began imagining something new—a new church driven by a particular mission. They would be Portland First's missionaries to the young adults of Portland who were uninterested in traditional churches. What would this new community look like? How would it be connected to Portland First? A church within a church? A church plant? Who would pastor this new missional gathering? They had no answers to these questions, and Mark wanted to keep it that way. He didn't see himself as the person who should be making those decisions. Rather, his role consisted of sharing the burden on his heart with the church, casting vision, and then making a way for something to happen.

With the support of the church board, Mark cast the vision for this new missionary church one Sunday morning during his sermon. He remembers feeling incredibly nervous, with no idea about how the congregation would respond. Not only was he asking them to ideologically support a mission without any details of what it would look like, but he was also asking for their financial support.

To their credit, the congregation responded courageously, demonstrating incredible faith in the unknown, release of control over the outcome, and remarkable financial support. Portland First raised $200,000 to support the mission of a community who would do what they couldn't do on their own. This seed money would cover the salary of a full-time pastor/missionary for a two-year period as well as provide the new mission with startup money. The remainder of the money at the end of the two-year period would become the new church's savings.

Hiring a Missionary to Portland

After setting aside money for the new community, Portland First began the search for the person who would come to lead this endeavor. They hoped for a pastor with a missionary heart and a passion for young adults. They wanted a mature pastor, who would not simply tolerate the parent church (Portland First) but who would actually love them for who they are. The pastor needed to be a dreamer, willing to try new things, while taking risks with the possibility of failure. Lastly, the pastor had to be up for anything and everything. After all, they were bringing on this pastor to do *something*, and this leader would guide the discernment of what God imagined that *something* to be.

Portland First found Pastor Jason Veach through a district superintendent who knew what they were looking for and thought Jason might be a good fit. Mark told Jason to come with the vision of a church planter. That planted church might remain a ministry of Portland First or take on a life of its own. No matter the form the community might take or how it might eventually connect to the parent church, Portland First planned that this new community would need to be self-sustaining after a period of two years. Jason and his family moved from the Midwest to Portland in July 2011, eager to get connected and to discover what God was already doing in Portland. Jason spent his first six months serving on the staff of Portland First with the title "new community pastor." Jason began by meeting with people—building relationships, making connections, and having as many conversations as possible—to get a pulse on where to begin. When sharing coffee or lunch with someone, Jason asked questions like:

- What does the church need to look like to reach this generation?
- What *is* the church, really?
- What are the essentials?
- What is nonessential or cultural?
- What can stay the same?
- What needs to drastically change?

These questions and the answers he heard helped him develop vision for what would become Eden Community.[1]

With the encouragement of Pastor Mark, he also asked these questions of several members of Portland First. He even made announcements in worship on a few Sundays, catching people up on what he had been up to and inviting those who might be interested in joining this new community to come to one of the question-and-answer sessions he hosted. Following Q&A sessions, Jason began to get a sense of which Portland First members were sensing a call to take the next step to commit to this new community.

From there, Jason held a series of meetings they called Core. For members of Portland First who'd expressed interest in joining the new community, attending Core was the next step. The focus of Core shifted from week to week. Some weeks, the focus was worship, teaching, and prayer. Other weeks, community building, service, and outreach took center stage. One goal of Core was to lay a foundation for starting the ministry and provide a context to begin living into the vision. Nothing was off the table at Core. Starting at the beginning, they tried to strip away what they already knew about following Jesus and being part of a church. With those ideas and experiences set aside, they could ask, "What really matters? What shape will this community take?"

Launching a Missionary Church

It became increasingly clear to Jason that the new community Portland First had envisioned years earlier would take the form of a church plant. Mark and Jason worked to define the relationship between Portland First and this new faith community, now named Eden Community Church. They developed a document to help share the vision for Eden Community with the whole congregation at Portland First. They described Eden Community as a parent-affiliated church (Portland First being the parent). The two congregations would be "connected yet distinct." Eden Community was a church plant while still being an extension of the ministry of Portland First. Being careful to affirm both ministries as valuable for kingdom work, they explained:

Launching this new ministry is not as simple as just offering another worship service at a different time of the week. The language, culture, lifestyles, and assumptions of new generations are different from the generations that precede them. This calls for some different paradigms of ministry to be employed and a missionary approach to be taken. This is why we have consistently said that this new ministry is not another program to be added. It is a new, mission-focused community with approaches and strategies of ministry that may differ from PFCN's existing ministries. This does not mean one is wrong and another right. Far from it! It does mean, however, that different kinds of communities are needed to reach different people.[2]

On the Sunday before Eden Community had their first separate worship service, the two congregations had a final joint service. The prayer time included a commissioning litany, where members of both churches had the opportunity respond to these commitments: to be faithful disciples of Christ, to be faithful to the mission of Christ's church, and to pursue unity in the faith even as we celebrate the diversity that exists among us. A prayer of commissioning and blessing for Eden Community followed the responsive litany.

Eden could not have happened without the vision and innovation of this traditional congregation, who took a risk by stepping into this holy discontent. Portland First responded to God's missional call financially before Jason ever came on the scene. The church then responded by sharing space: Eden met for four years in Portland First's building, some of that time without paying rent. Portland First also responded relationally by sending some of their own members to make up the core that covenanted to plant Eden.

Eden Community eventually evolved into a full church plant that became independent of its parent church. While there were many people, Mark among them, who hoped the two congregations could remain connected in some way, they had to make the choice that was best for the mission of Eden Community. From the beginning, Mark clearly stated to the congregation: "We don't know what this mission will become. We are building the wagon as we go. It could be a ministry of Portland First. It could be a church within a church. It could be a church plant. We have to be willing to give this new congregation the most autonomy possible. Every decision has to be based on the mission."[3]

Eden began paying rent to Portland First for use of their multipurpose space in 2013, even before Portland First asked for it. Eden Community's leadership team thought paying rent would help them make the transition to a more realistic budget, since rent or a mortgage would be an inevitable budget consideration in the future. Portland First graciously offered the rent on a sliding scale so that the price began very low but gradually increased over time. By the time they moved out of the building, Eden Community was paying the same rate as any other outside group who rented the space.

Despite Portland First's courageous investment in the unknown, and despite Jason and Mark's best efforts to prepare their people for the next steps, when it finally came time for the congregations to meet separately, Jason felt they had under-communicated what this would mean. It was one thing for members of Portland First to express support for those beloved church members who sensed a call to be part of the new community. But it was a whole different, and much harder, thing to actually say goodbye. Once the realization set in that those who remained at Portland First wouldn't be seeing people they loved every Sunday, people became confused. Those they had commissioned were called and were leaving— but for how long? For good? Forever? Mark feels that casting a vision as you go will inevitably lead to some confusion since the outcome remains unknown through the process.

Eden Community began meeting separately from Portland First with a Sunday evening service in the spring of 2012. Over the next two years, they explored possibilities for continued connection with Portland First while experiencing the positive pressure to become a self-sustaining ministry and church plant. Eden maintained connection with Portland First through occasional joint worship events, partnering in service projects at a local public school, and offering joint discipleship and Christian education classes. However, the fact that the two congregations worshiped at different times made meeting together a logistical challenge. Eden Community found that staying connected to Portland First required time and energy that, in some cases, pulled Eden away from their mission—the very mission on which Portland First had sent them.

In the spring of 2015, Jason met with the Portland First board to determine the next steps for Eden's identity. He proposed that Eden organize as an independent church, knowing his own board had been ready to make this move for the last year. He put the decision in Portland First's hands, acknowledging that it was their investment in Eden Community in the first place and their incredible faith and sharing of resources that had birthed this new church and mission. The Portland First board unanimously voted to release Eden Community from the parent-

Parent-Affiliated Church Planting

For established churches considering becoming a parent church of a plant, Pastor Mark cautions to do so only after strongly communicating a readiness to release control and valuable leaders to the new mission. The senior pastor of the parent church must completely trust the pastor who comes in to lead the new church. If the senior pastor can't release control, then the parent church is not yet ready for this endeavor.

The parent church also must prepare to give members from the parent congregation to the new congregation. This involves risk because there will inevitably be holes in leadership roles as talented people leave the parent church. Once again, if the parent church is not ready to take this risk, then the church is not ready to plant.

affiliated relationship. The board gathered around Jason to pray a prayer of blessing and affirmation for the future mission of the church. Following that meeting, Eden Community—full of gratitude for Portland First's remarkable investment—became a fully independent church. Portland First took great risks to support a people who didn't yet exist and a mission that hadn't fully formed. Eden was the tree that grew from the seed of Portland First's faith.

Ministry Rhythms and Development

Church planters treasure the blank canvas of a new church. They get the privilege of experimenting, dreaming, and listening without any ties to the way things have always been done. One of the first items on the Eden Community to-do list for Jason was to shape the space for Sunday worship, and he had a blank slate. They began meeting in a café space on one of the lower levels in Portland First's building. It's a large room that easily divides into different areas. A coffee bar greets people immediately as they walk in. Just past the café area sit foosball and pool tables. For the gathered portion of worship, they set up chairs near the end of the room, situated around some of the sacred symbols. They celebrate the Eucharist weekly, so the table is always at the forefront, along with a cross and a basin of water for baptismal remembrance.

Eden has always met in flexible space, and that mobility and flexibility was intentionally part of their DNA. One Core member explains, "We wanted to be able to be mobile. We didn't want to be so tied to a space." Eden practices this mobility by meeting in different locations for worship throughout the year. Though, at the beginning, they primarily met in the café space at Portland First, they also take Sundays for service projects, and they'll meet at the site of that Sunday's project. Eden has also experimented with church in the park, church on the hiking trail, and meeting every Sunday during July and August in an outdoor amphitheater on the grounds of Portland First.

Eden intentionally works beyond the walls of the church. The posture they chose from the beginning demonstrates their philosophy of ministry: "We're not called to save Portland but to serve Portland."[4] Instead of acting on the impulse to start something new, they decided early on that they would join with others in the good work already being done. Jason believes this approach to ministry outside the church reinforces their posture of service, and it's also easier. A new church, busy with forming

Innovation: Serve Sundays

Eden has a regular rhythm of devoting one or two Sundays a year for service, which they call "Worship+Service." In place of the normal worship gathering, they gather onsite at a nonprofit or a location where another service project is taking place in the community. The pastoral staff use intentional language surrounding this day and work. Serving doesn't replace worship; rather, service *is* an act of worship.

Eden Community embraces the flexible body of Christ. Since the church is the body of people, it is baffling that so many congregations are tied down to the same worship location week after week. The church—the body of Christ—can worship anywhere.

How often does someone wander into your church building on a Sunday? For many churches, that's rare. This innovative approach to church as the mobile-ly gathered body of Christ, instead of church as a building, frees Eden Community to live into who God calls the church to be in the world.

identity and creating new rhythms, doesn't need to do the hard work of starting a second ministry, especially when many people are already doing great work in the community.

In many cases, Eden Community has established partnerships through a conversation between Jason and a representative from a particular nonprofit. With a desire to learn and listen, Jason often says, "Tell me about your mission." Then he asks, "How do you see a church like ours helping you accomplish that mission?" The innovative shift occurs in how Eden approaches these partnerships. Instead of telling an organization, "We have an idea for how we can help you," Eden says to the organization, "You tell us how we can help you." One cannot underestimate the importance of a shift like this. Churches who approach service outside the walls with this kind of attitude develop remarkably different relationships with their partners in ministry.

Jason sees himself as a community mobilizer; his job is to send people out. When parishioners or small groups want to serve outside the church, he tries to send them to places where they can join the work people are already doing. By maintaining partnerships with several organizations, he's able to make recommendations after discerning where the resources or skills of individuals or groups intersect with how a given organization has answered the question, "Tell us how we can help you."

In addition to shaping their space of worship and their posture of service, Eden Community embraced the opportunity to mold the worship gathering with care and intent. They integrate many traditional elements of liturgy during service: call to worship, songs of praise, corporate prayer, preached Word, passing the peace, Communion, and a benediction. No matter where they gather, worship moves through the same basic rhythm from week to week. But Eden innovates within this weekly rhythm by providing tactile opportunities for the whole congregation, both to participate in worship and to respond to the preached Word. Weekly Communion offers the invitation to come to the Table and partake of the bread and juice, taking Christ's body into one's own body. On the way to the Communion Table, one can also dip a finger in the baptismal font (a silver basin of water placed centrally in front of the table) and mark the sign of the cross on the forehead, to remember one's baptism and baptismal vows. Just after receiving Communion, members

---

Innovation: Embracing the Arts in Worship

Eden Community goes out of its way to incorporate the arts in their worship gatherings. Here are a few examples:

- During a sermon series on the "I Am" passages from John, members could come forward following Communion to record what they were learning on a card and pin it on an artfully made board with others' responses. The card said, "Because Christ is . . . I am _____."
- One Pentecost Sunday, members wrote their prayers on colored fabrics that were attached to a frame, creating a communal art piece.
- Film interviews, visual liturgy, and video pieces, both made in house and produced by The Work of the People.
- Interactive prayer stations.
- During a sermon series on the parables, members planted seed pots together, took them home, and reported back about their progress.
- Using drama and reader's theater.
- One creative member designs artistic, devotional and/or discussion booklets to serve as guides for discussion or journaling that follow the current sermon series.

---

have the option of stopping at a prayer station, situated off to the side, to light a candle for someone they want to lift up to God in prayer.

Although these tactile responses are not uncommon for some traditions, Eden Community takes innovation a step further by also celebrating and integrating the arts during worship. Often, they provide a tactile response to the preached Word through various artistic expressions. A commissioned photography installation for the seasons of Advent and Lent is projected on the screens throughout the service and displayed on canvases in the worship space. One All Saints' Sunday, members made small crosses that displayed the name of their chosen saint. Later, all of those crosses were plastered to one large cross that reappears year after year, reminding the congregation of the continual witness of the saints and displaying this communal piece of art.

Moving into a New (Permanent?) Space

Eden Community continued to meet for worship in the multipurpose café space at Portland First until 2016. In 2015, when Eden Community officially organized as an independent church, they decided they needed to begin looking for a new space to worship. They loved their space at PFCN, but it wasn't easy to find in the huge building, and the church building wasn't located near a residential neighborhood. The people Eden Community wants to see come to Christ already have many walls and barriers keeping them from getting in the doors of a church. Eden's leaders felt that merely *finding* the worship space shouldn't be one more barrier.

Jason formed a team to begin searching for a new space. They did some groundwork, assessing their own community, culture, and needs. During worship one week, Jason had the congregation divide into small groups to answer the question, "What breaks your heart in our city?" They compiled this list, believing that the space where they would choose to root themselves should also align with these passions and heartaches. With a good sense of what they needed and a list of the areas that already captured their passions, the search team drafted a wish list for what they hoped they'd find. They scoured Portland's exorbitant real estate market for more than a year. They brainstormed different options for how to make an expensive space more affordable and collaborative, considering sharing a lease with other churches or nonprofits. As lead after lead collapsed, the whole process began to feel depressing.

After a year of searching, finally an opportunity opened up for a lease at a school only three miles from PFC. However, there were some caution signals. The leadership team had serious concerns about meeting in a school. Setting up and tearing down each week would require a massive time investment, and installing the necessary audiovisual equipment could be prohibitively expensive. Slowly, each obstacle resolved one after another, through God's provision and the hospitality of Hope Chinese Charter School. The school even helped pay for a sound system and projection equipment. Further, the context of a school and the location put them in touch with almost every major theme marked by their passions for Portland. It is clear to the whole community that Hope Chinese Charter School is where God has called Eden Community to root itself for this season of their ministry and mission.

Already in the rhythm of Service Sundays, Eden Community embraced the posture of service for two consecutive Sundays as they prepared to move. They had equipment to move and quite a bit of work to do to prepare their space. But they also asked the school for any suggestions or input on projects they needed done, so both groups benefited from these service days. The principal longed for a social gathering outside the weekly grind, where parents, teachers, and students could get together. The school had no community activities scheduled during the fall semester. On the other hand, Eden was already planning to host a fall festival to help their new neighbors know about their presence in the school. Eden transformed the festival they were planning into what the school needed, which gave Eden another opportunity to invest in the new partnership, and it gave the school's families a chance to meet the new tenants.

Once Eden Community had finally fully settled into the new space at the end of 2016, they felt able to take a breath. With the question of space and location resolved, they were able to focus on beginning to grow roots in the neighborhood and build on their partnership with the school. They also hope to become a more diverse community now that the church is located in a more multicultural area. Eden Community continues doing the work of the church through worship and service, and they remain committed to discovering and living out through mission what God dreams for their future.

Learn More

- http://edenpdx.org
- Interview with Pastor Jason on *This Nazarene Life*, produced by Brit Bolerjack; Season 1, Episode 13, http://thisnazlife.com/2016/09/12/ep-13-rev-jason-veach/

Recommended Resources:

- *Marks of the Missional Church: Ecclesial Practices for the Sake of the World,* by Keith Schwanz, Libby Tedder Hugus, and Jason Veach (2014)
- *The Shaping of Things to Come: Innovation and Mission for the 21st-Century Church,* by Michael Frost and Alan Hirsch (2003)
- *Mission-shaped Church: Church Planting and Fresh Expressions in a Changing Context*, published by the Church of England's Mission and Public Affairs Council (2004)
- "Religion among the Millennials," Pew Research Center, http://www.pewforum.org/2010/02/17/religion-among-the-millennials

Discussion Questions

1. Is your church in a position to consider planting a new congregation through the parent-affiliated model? Is this something God might be calling you to do?

2. Has your church ever considered being mobile for a Sunday? If you've thought about it but not gone through with it, what has stopped you? If not, would you be willing to try it?

3. List the partnerships your church has with other organizations or projects. Who sets the agenda—your church or the partner organization?

4. What tactile participation or responses are currently part of your worship service?

5. How does your congregation embrace the arts?

6. Does the physical space where your church gathers match your church's mission? What are the barriers for people to get into your worship space? What can you do to lessen those barriers?

12

The Church Where Nobody Knows What's Going On

Name: Church in Action

Denomination: Church of the Nazarene

Location: Frankfurt, Germany

Size: Large (700)

Ethnic Makeup: 70% German; 15% Middle Eastern; 5% African; 5% American; 5% Asian

"I WANTED to be the German Billy Graham," explains Philip Zimmermann. "But then one of my professors told me that only 1 percent of converts at Billy Graham crusades were still involved in churches ten years later. I found that to be really discouraging, so I thought I should go into church planting if I really wanted to see people transformed." With that in mind, Philip planted a church in 2008 in Mainz, Germany. Mainz is a city of about 200,000 that sits southwest of Frankfurt along the Rhine River. Since 2008, Church in Action has become a shockingly innovative church with so many things going on that they can't even count them. When asked to get specific about numbers, Philip usually looks out into space and says something along the lines of: "I'm not sure how many we have now." When pressed, he comes up with sixteen worship services, around forty ministry sites in four cities, and somewhere in the neighborhood of one thousand people involved in one way or another. So how did they get from a tiny church plant to an organic, missional explosion? No one really saw this coming, but the growth happened in four distinct phases—five if you count the pre-work.

Phase 0: Conversion to the Kingdom

Philip grew up in the Church of the Nazarene. His grandfather Richard Zanner was the first German district superintendent and, later, the regional director for Africa. Philip's father was also a Nazarene pastor. When Philip was growing up in Germany, the gospel he heard explained was: "God is good. You are bad. You need to ask God to forgive you so you can go to heaven." Philip and his brother, Cris, were not particularly interested in this form of religion. However, because of their family history, they stayed connected to the church. Eventually, they both reconnected with Christ and both felt called to full-time ministry. Philip was passionate about helping people connect with God, so he preached in revival services across Europe and held altar calls—"the whole shebang," he says.

After he graduated from Bible college, he knew he wanted to plant a church. He was influenced by Bill Hybels and Rick Warren, and he wanted to give his life to one place for the long haul. But then Philip experienced what he calls his second conversion: "I was converted to the person of Jesus when I became a Christian, and I was converted to the message of Jesus when I began to think about what Jesus really meant when he said he was proclaiming the kingdom of God." Up to this point, Philip hadn't actually heard much about the kingdom. Even though he had studied theology for four years and listened to thousands of sermons, somehow he had never heard the kingdom of God explained. Philip was shocked to discover that Jesus's central message was not forgiveness or love or even reconciliation. Rather, the single theme that unites Jesus's teachings in the Bible is this mysterious kingdom of God. This realization was a cataclysmic paradigm shift for Philip. He realized that the foundational question is "'What is the kingdom of God?' If church leaders get this question wrong, they get a distorted view of almost everything else concerning Christianity."[1]

Through his studies, Philip developed a working definition of the kingdom of God as heaven on earth. Jesus taught his disciples to pray, "your kingdom come, your will be done, on earth as it is in heaven" (Matthew 6:10), so Philip explains that God's desire "is that whatever happens in heaven also transpires here on earth . . . The kingdom of God is not just something in the future; it is God's shalom breaking into our midst, into our lives, into our mess and chaos. God starts to heal, to set free, to forgive, and to put back together what is broken in our world."[2]

Reclaiming the kingdom of God as the central message of Christianity revolutionized Philip's ecclesiology. He began to see that "the church is just a means to an end, not the end itself. We realized that God is interested in all aspects of society. God wants to see all the places of your city where the shalom of God is not yet a reality. God wants us to set up signposts of the new creation in our city and in our world." If the gospel and the church are all about the kingdom, then "the calling of the church is to proclaim and live out heaven on earth. The church is a community of people that experiences, announces, and passes on the in-breaking shalom of God."[3]

Philip muses, "Jesus proclaimed a revolution with the kingdom of God to turn this world into the world it ought to be, and we made a Sunday morning worship service out it. The number of people in our pews became the measurement of our success, whereas Jesus dreamed of a whole new world, a better world, a heaven on earth. God is not just interested in getting people into heaven but in getting heaven to break out on earth. That changed everything for us."

Phase 1: Startup

In 2008, while still in his twenties, Philip gathered a hundred volunteers (seventy-five Americans and twenty-five Germans) for Project Camp. For one week, they had a major outreach push in Mainz. Every day they facilitated service projects, concerts, and an evangelistic sermon. Every night they cooked dinner in a big tent downtown for two hundred people. After this weeklong burst of momentum, Philip and his core group invited people to join them for a worship service in a bar. Because they served a meal beforehand, a large contingent of homeless people became part of their community.

However, Church in Action only held these services every two weeks. "We decided we don't want to put 90 percent of our resources into a one-hour event," Philip explains. "This enabled us to say that serving the community is not just a program next to the worship service but is actually just as important as what the church does in our communal gatherings. Small groups are not just an add-on but are really at the heart of the church. We didn't want people to spend all their time with Christians. We wanted people to have time to be involved in culture, the whole idea of incarnation. We wanted people to see that there is a balance."

Within the first six months, Church in Action (which embraces the ironic acronym of CIA) solidified a vision informed by Philip's conversion to kingdom-centric theology: "We want to see heaven break into our lives, our city, and our world." (They regularly tell success stories on social media with the hashtag #HeavenOnEarth.) For them, heaven breaks in through four key missional concepts.

Share is about being part of the lives of others who do not belong to the church. "A church should not hide from the world but, rather, live incarnated as the body of Christ in it."[4] In addition to investing deeply into the lives of others through work, hobby groups, sports clubs, and cultural events, CIA converted an old hotel into a communal living space where Christians and non-Christians could share life together.

Excite is focused on inspiring passion for Jesus through corporate worship services. Even though CIA intentionally invests the majority of their time, energy, and money in events outside the weekend worship service, they still believe corporate worship plays a key role in wooing people to passionate commitment to Jesus.

Grow is focused on discipleship through small groups and mentoring. One reason for having corporate worship biweekly is to make space for small groups to meet in the alternating weeks. Deep discipleship simply can't happen without deep community.

Serve is about investing ourselves to help our community and our world. CIA knew right from the beginning that the church exists for people who are not part of it and perhaps never will be part of it. They started with what they call impact projects, where they ask, "Where can we bring a piece of heaven into the world?"

The vision was working, in part. Church in Action was a beautiful mix of homeless people, students, and social workers. On the other hand, many new people came for a while, said, "This is how church *should* be,"

Rethinking Church Planting

"Often when we think of church planting," says Philip, "we think of planting worship services, and we think that once we have planted a worship service, we have planted a church. This is just stupid from a theological point of view." Church in Action still holds all sixteen of their worship services on a biweekly basis for three reasons.

1) It affirms that the church is more than the worship hour and gives space for growth groups and service projects.

2) A biweekly rotation keeps people healthily unsettled. "You don't get as much commitment," says Philip, "but the community stays more open to new people."

3) Church in Action can connect with more people in more locations.

and then eventually moved on to other churches. Philip admits, "It's hard to worship next to a homeless person who just peed his pants."

All of Philip's education and training told him that his job was to expand his worship service, but they just couldn't grow beyond fifty to sixty people. For a few years, Philip felt frustrated and consistently stymied. In 2011, CIA bought a coffee shop in Mainz and shifted their worship services to that location. However, they still couldn't break through to the next level. Looking back, Philip says his biggest mistake was focusing his energy on trying to grow this one particular service in one particular style. Eventually, he was able to appreciate this unique mix of believers as a beautiful—if limited—expression of church. Without trying to change what they had, they began to envision something new.

Phase 2: Multiple Services

Meanwhile, Philip's brother, Cris Zimmermann, was pastoring Frankfurt First Church of the Nazarene, about thirty miles away. Slowly, Cris became more and more frustrated because he couldn't innovate enough in that traditional context. In 2010, Cris planted a church in Frankfurt, also called Church in Action, and with the same basic DNA as his brother's Mainz plant. For the first two years, they met in a local bar with no worship services at all. They were incarnational missionaries becoming embedded into a new community where there was no active Christian presence. For more than a hundred weeks, their goal was simply to build redemptive relationships with the people who frequented that bar. In one of CIA's recent vlogs, Cris reflects on this concept as he walks around downtown San Diego:

> I've just come out of a number of meetings with pastors and leaders. We've been doing some brainstorming and thinking about: What does it mean to be the church in the twenty-first century? How can we reach millennials? How do we enter the large cities? But the question I'm asking myself today is not "How can we get life into church?" but "How can we get church into life?" Because I'm just walking through the city here this morning, and there's so much life happening in the restaurants and the pubs and the bars and the coffee shops. It seems like lots of people here in California are enjoying life, and I also assume that there are lots of people in church this morning. Of course, we could try to get more people into church, but how about getting church into life?[5]

Church in Action has thrived in large part because they have deeply lived their mission of sharing life with people outside the church. Longtime member Andreas Lemperle says this is why he loves CIA: "This model of living out one's beliefs has encouraged me from the first day. When people don't come to the church, we have to go to them."

CIA City Pastor Eric Smith sounds distinctly like a missionary as he describes their strategy when entering a new space. They have "the vision of building relationships, of incarnational ministry, learning how people talk these days, learning what moves people these days. How do they live? What is their culture like?"[6]

In 2012, Cris's new church bought a coffee shop in Frankfurt and finally started a simple worship service there. Next, recognizing that the elderly are often lonely and ignored, they began a worship service in a nursing home. After that, they began multiplying worship services in a variety of locations and contexts. This multiplication was Cris's key innovation. He saw that you don't have to keep everyone together. You can run parallel events with different focal points. They have discovered that each location reaches some new people who wouldn't have come to the other locations.

In each new setting, CIA is careful to craft the event to the local context. Philip explains, "We don't have one style, but actually we have a lot of different styles of how we do worship. It's kind of user-centric. In an elderly home, it's very traditional. In a coffee shop it's very laid back. In a theater, it's very high-end production. For us, it's all a means to an end—for that group of people to connect with God."

Hosting a worship service isn't their first step, though; it is typically their third or fourth. Instead, they usually start with simply getting to know people. Then they begin a justice-oriented ministry or a social gathering. After these steps have built credibility and cultivated some interest, they start a worship service. They don't worry too much about critical mass. They just get started. In Frankfurt, for example, they began a ministry in a nightlife bar that was only open from 6:00 p.m. to 5:00 a.m. Their entry point was hosting charity events. The bar owner is Ethiopian, so CIA's first event was a fundraiser for a water well in Africa. They were able to borrow on the owner's relational capital, and he was able to give back to where he came from. That combination enabled them to get started in a new location.

According to Eric, CIA is constantly asking: "Where are people already gathering? How can we reconnect with people? Where are people naturally, organically meeting?" For more than a year after CIA began ministry in Darmstadt (about twenty miles from both Mainz and Frankfurt), they felt led to one of the city's premier bars. But the owners "didn't want anything to do with Christians or with church." A year later, CIA asked again, and this time, not only did the owners open the doors to the church, but the bar also advertised the opening event on its website and Facebook page. On launch night, more than a hundred people showed up—more than twice the number of seats available. Eric glows as he shares this testimony on a CIA vlog: "It's crazy to think that sometimes it takes a year for a door to open. God opens doors all the time, and we just have to trust and follow."[7]

Phase 3: Merger and Innovation Overload

In 2014, the Frankfurt and Mainz CIAs merged into one, unified church with multiple campuses, and they began ministry in two nearby cities: Darmstadt and Wiesbaden. Philip and Cris became co-pastors of the unified church. This structural shift opened the floodgates for innovation.

But this was progress birthed out of pain. "If I'm honest," admits Philip, "that merger came out of my own personal frustration." He realized that the little church in Mainz, while beautiful and missional, had moved into maintenance mode. Philip is an incurable entrepreneur-apostle. He always has the itch to start new things and to make them grow. Cris was planting various congregations in multiple locations throughout Frankfurt, so they decided to work together to try this strategy in Mainz and the surrounding area. Before the merger, the two churches were already doing creative work, but coming together enabled a synergy to emerge from Cris and Philip's partnership in ministry. They have the same philosophy of ministry and complementary gifts. Cris is more pastoral, and Philip is more strategic. Philip gives oversight to the project-based ministries, and Cris guides and mentors the city pastors, who are in charge of all the worship services and pastoral care in each of the four cities.

Setting Philip and Cris free to excel in their own areas of strength was like pouring gasoline on the fire. Since 2014, their ministries have sprouted like dandelions. They have sixteen different worship services spread around four cities in the Rhine-Main valley, meeting in coffee shops, bars, nursing homes, restaurants, movie theaters, and hospitals. They have dozens and dozens of missional ministry sites serving refugees, the homeless, the elderly, and prostitutes.

Both Cris and Philip are happy entrepreneurs. As they set out on this wild innovation phase, they tried to approach it in a relaxed way: "If it works, great. If it doesn't work, that's okay. Let's try to make some disciples in the meantime." Philip says they consciously took on a startup mentality: "We tried to embrace this lean process, where you can fail and fail fast. Just go ahead. So we are always in the starting business. If we have a week when we don't start something new or hire a new person, it feels like the week was lost."

Getting this innovation train started wasn't easy, though. Many experiments just didn't work. Especially at the beginning, it was hard to figure out how to start new gatherings in new locations. Even now, they still have nightmares about standing up to preach in front of an empty pub. On the bright side, Philip says, "The nice thing about meeting in small spaces is that twenty to thirty people feels full." But Philip sees those early growing pains as part of the learning process: "It was very difficult for us at the beginning. Now we start new things much more easily."

A few of Church in Action's unique ministries are worth highlighting.

First, since 2015, CIA teams have been going into local brothels every week because, as Eric says, "the church *has* to be where the city's greatest need is."[8] Volunteers visit red-light districts and offer simple gifts like makeup or homemade cookies to prostitutes to express love and to serve as an icebreaker for further conversation. The volunteers listen to their stories, pray with them, give them Bibles and other literature in their native languages, and help them connect with professional services like doctors, counselors, and social workers. When the women are ready, the volunteers connect them with public programs to provide a way out of the sex industry.

Second, CIA has been working among refugees since 2010. However, with Germany receiving more than a million refugees in 2015 alone, both the needs and the opportunities have grown exponentially. The German government meets the refugees' basic needs like food, clothing, and shelter, so the greatest needs are relational connection and a sense of purpose.

For nearly a century, the Western church has sent missionaries to the Middle East at great cost and great personal risk, and usually with little fruit to show for their efforts. Now, millions of people from closed countries are flooding into Europe, and they are desperate for hope. This is a wide-open door for the church, and CIA is running through that door. With funding from World Vision and Nazarene Compassionate Ministries, CIA created a *Spielmobil* (play car)—a customized van packed with games for kids of all ages and a mobile coffee shop—to visit the refugee camps. At each camp, they set up game stations for kids, with toys specifically chosen to help develop motor and communication skills. The coffee bar allows the parents to have a hot drink and chat with volunteers while they watch their kids play. The goal is to develop long-term relationships with these families. CIA has seen dozens and dozens of refugees come to faith in Christ through this effort, and many refugees now volunteer with the *Spielmobil* and other ministries as translators, cooks, and even as pastors of refugee congregations.

When CIA discovered that many of the refugees in their area were actually professional musicians, CIA assembled Bridges, a combined orchestra of Germans and refugees. After the first concert played to eight hundred people and aired on German TV, various smaller ensembles have played dozens of concerts all across Germany.

Finally, the entire church closes down its normal programs and services each summer for a six-week-long missional sabbatical. They send short-term mission teams all over the world. In 2016, they sent out 150 people across ten teams to ten different countries. Interestingly, 20 to 30 percent of the mission team participants are not Christians, so CIA calls these "mission mission" trips. This practice is part of their overall philosophy to let people belong before they start to believe. As soon as visitors enter a CIA space, they immediately belong. Then the church simply invites them on the journey of following Jesus in serving others even if they don't fully understand it all.

Eric explains, "Surprisingly, even in Europe, people are up for doing good for others. It is easy to invite people to do good."[9] Through the process of living embedded in Christian community and doing good for others, people encounter God in new ways without even realizing what is happening. Slowly, they enter the faith journey and ask questions. Eric says, "We see it over and over and over again. As they join the journey, through the power of the Holy Spirit and through time, they come to the place of believing, of saying, 'I want to follow Christ. I want to step into baptism.'"[10]

As CIA has blossomed, Cris and Philip have realized that, even though they are great at starting things, they need more structure. An architect who has been part of CIA for five years meets with Philip every week to develop better systems of management and measurement. They have a

---

Polity Innovations

One key to facilitating innovation is flexible structures. The German district of the Church of the Nazarene has allowed a few key polity innovations so that this new, growing plant wouldn't be held back by an old flower pot.

1. *CIA doesn't have membership.* After taking in the required minimum of members to be officially organized as a church under German law, CIA hasn't added a single official member. There are two reasons for this. First, in a highly entrepreneurial setting, they just don't have the time or emotional energy to manage the system normally involved in church governance. Second, they don't want to set up any checkpoints that would serve as barriers for people to draw closer to Jesus.

2. *In 2016, CIA officially became categorized as a partner organization to the German district rather than a local church.* As CIA has multiplied ministries in urban centers, it made the most sense for the district to classify them as a training partner. In terms of their internal identity, though, CIA still thinks of themselves as a local church. They are also committed to maintaining their Nazarene identity. All their assistant pastors are going through the ordination track with the Church of the Nazarene.

huge whiteboard with an outline of all of their ministries and three hundred little magnets with pictures of the faces of their volunteers. Each week they move around the magnets, trying to get an accurate picture of who is doing what and where and with whom. The refugee ministry is exploding so quickly that it is particularly hard to keep track of. Every week when he leaves, the architect says about one project or another, "I learned something new today. I didn't even know we were doing that."

After telling this story, Philip laughed and said, "We actually have no idea what all is happening."

Phase 4: Teaching Site

Starting a sprawling, multi-site church that is spread over four cities and across several languages, and reaching people whom few other churches even try to touch, are not enough for Cris and Philip Zimmermann. They are on a mission to reform both church and mission—or, maybe more accurately stated, to reunite church and mission—in a way that literally transforms our world.

Philip laments, "Five hundred years ago the church was on the innovative edge with the arts and architecture. We used to say that the church is twenty to thirty years behind culture, but that is no longer true. Our culture is increasing the pace of change, but the church is not. Now, the gap between the church and the culture is increasing every year. We are getting further and further behind." But Philip remains optimistic. "I think we can turn the ship around. I think the Catholic Church was wise in creating different orders and giving innovative leaders freedom to operate within different streams. We don't all need to change, but we need the freedom to change if we feel called to that."

As Cris and Philip look toward the future, of course they want to help CIA continue to expand and to transform the Frankfurt area. Even more, however, they want to become an incubation center for urban ministries. Nazarene churches have often struggled in our big cities around the world, particularly in Europe and North America. To address this need, CIA has begun the Urban Transformation master's program in partnership with Nazarene Theological College in Manchester, England. It's an intense, two-and-half-year journey that combines ministry classes and practical work at CIA. "It is designed to equip a new generation of mature, Christian leaders to transform cities by planting churches and serving effectively in postmodern, post-Christian, urban environments."

Through this program, CIA aims to raise up a generation of young European leaders who can establish vibrant Christian communities in cities across Europe.

CIA is also sharing what they've learned by inviting teams from around the world to join them for short-term mission-learning trips. These visits give people the opportunity to lend a hand in special events, to learn, and to be inspired to reach out to their own communities in similar ways.

The Church in Action team members know they are in the midst of a massive experiment. While Eric was speaking at a leadership event once, someone asked him about CIA's five-year plan. He chuckled and said, "You know, I'm not even sure we have a one-day plan. Of course, we have vision and strategy for where we want to go, but we just continue to look for need. Then we try to go meet that need in whatever way we can, just day by day, taking another step, and trying to redeem everything for him."[11]

Learn More

- Check out the vlogs and read more about CIA's ecclesiology with the free download "7 Words That Define the Missional Church" at http://churchinaction.com/7-words-landing-page.
- Browse CIA's internal website, which has a more complete listing of ministries and locations, at http://www.kircheinaktion.de/en.
- Listen to an interview with Eric Smith, a CIA city pastor, on the *This Nazarene Life* podcast (Season 1, Episode 12), http://thisnazlife.com/2016/08/29/ep-12-pastor-eric-smith/

Discussion Questions

1. Philip says he had a second conversion when he came to understand the kingdom of God. Does your church talk much about the kingdom? Do you agree that the kingdom of God is at the core of Jesus's central message? If it is, what does that mean for the church?

2. Once Church in Action got rolling, they had something beautiful and missional, but they stalled at about fifty to sixty people. One of their big lessons learned was that different people need different worship styles and locations. Are there people or places near you where a different worship style might fit?

3. CIA deeply values sharing life with non-Christians and engaging in secular cultural events, but many other churches become "Christian ghettos," where Christians are isolated from their surrounding culture. How does your church do with encouraging positive cultural engagement? How many of your close friends are outside the church?

4. Often, church rules and denominational structures can be stifling for innovators like Cris and Philip. Instead of considering them dangerous mavericks, however, the German district for the Church of the Nazarene gave them wide freedom. How can we make our churches and districts more welcome to people who want to try new things?

5. Philip spent two years visiting a local bar to learn the culture before he started a worship service there. How well do you know the culture of people nearby your church? How much time have you spent listening and asking questions like a cultural anthropologist?

13

A Word of Caution: The Dark Side of Innovation

HOPEFULLY you are both encouraged and inspired after having read these stories of innovation and breakthrough. The purpose of this project has always been to help pastors and church leaders reimagine the future and discover the courage to embrace the difficult work of being midwives as the Spirit causes the church to be born again. We believe wholeheartedly that God is doing something new in the global church and in our local churches, and we also believe that we can help.

Unfortunately, excitement and energy for such a mission can be short-lived. It can also be undermined by the difficulties inherent to the task. Therefore, we want to offer some words of caution to those who would boldly claim their place as kingdom pioneers. This is a book about failure, after all, but there's a big difference between failure that promotes innovation and failure that undercuts mission.

In naming this book, the challenge of innovation was made very clear to us. In the imagination of our culture, no figure readily embodies innovation quite like Thomas Edison. Thus, Edison made a perfect illustration of the process of failure toward innovation that we wanted to explore. However, Thomas Edison is also a perfect example of the dangers of the pursuit of innovation. In some ways, he is an example of what we hope *not* to become in the pursuit of the future of the church. In chasing the future, Thomas Edison was relentless and immensely self-focused. He not only developed new technologies that would change the world, but he also pursued wealth and personal glory. Edison was obsessed with his place in history, and his life was out of balance, filled with greed and self-importance.[1]

By all accounts, Edison was a disinterested husband and father. His greed and desire for notoriety pushed those around him to the margins of his focus. In his passion to show that his inventions were superior, he worked hard to discredit his competitors. One of the great battles of his life was the battle to get his DC (direct current) electrical grid to be the dominant source of power instead of Westinghouse's competing AC (alternating current). To demonstrate the dangers of AC power, Edison agreed to electrocute an elephant. The Luna Park Zoo in Coney Island was looking for a way to euthanize one of its elephants that had injured three of her handlers. Edison volunteered to kill the elephant and even filmed the execution via another of his inventions, a movie camera. Not only was this a barbaric act; it was also directly opposed to Edison's own stated morals as a vegetarian and pacifist.[2]

Innovation wasn't just a way for Edison to reshape the world and make his mark. It was an outlet for the worst parts of his ego and sinful nature. This downside is, unfortunately, a rather common occurrence for pioneers and innovators.

—⁂—

> **In the church, our passion for innovation and our willingness to endure failure must always be rooted in the ethos of the kingdom of God.**

—⁂—

Edisons in Our Churches

In the church, our passion for innovation and our willingness to endure failure must always be rooted in the ethos of the kingdom of God. God is not concerned only with outcomes. We do not pursue innovation by any means necessary. Jesus repeatedly had to rebuke his disciples when they tried to do what they thought were the right things by the wrong methods. Jesus was always as concerned with the process as he was with the results. In the kingdom of God, we cannot use people as a means to an end; people *are* the end.

Some innovators, intentionally or unintentionally, take the Parables of the Hidden Treasure and the Pearl (see Matthew 13) as permission to abandon anything and everyone in pursuit of the mission of the kingdom. They sacrifice their health, their families, and their relationships in pursuit of the work of God. In reality, however, life in the kingdom of God is always focused on how we live with and treat others. We see this when Jesus had to chastise the disciples for arguing about which of them would have the highest position of authority in the kingdom (see Mark 10). And in Luke 9, Jesus scolded the disciples for wishing harm on those who opposed them and for underestimating what it would cost them to take part in the work of God.

Throughout Scripture, we read stories of leaders who were called to do great things who, instead, compromised their calling and mission. They failed by not taking care of themselves, by not loving others well, or by choosing their own methods over God's. Consider Abram, tasked with the incredible responsibility of being the father of a great nation. As time dragged on and he saw no evidence that he would be the father of a child, much less a nation, he hurried God's timeline. Abram and Sarai decided he should father a child with their slave, Hagar. That child, Ishmael, became a painful lesson in trying to fast-forward God's plans. Ishmael, through no fault of his own, became a source of bitter pain for both Abram and Sarai. Our desire to speed up God's timing can give birth to a lot of Ishmaels—ideas that seemed great at the time but ultimately end up as tragedies and painful reminders of our inadequacy. Impatience is deeply destructive to the work of God.

Often, innovators feel the heavy weight of leadership on their shoulders. Moses learned the vital lesson of leadership reproduction and empowerment. It was his father-in-law, Jethro, who saw the way he was living and suggested a change. Moses saw himself as invaluable to the people and put an unnecessary burden on himself to arbitrate all their disputes. But Jethro saw the truth and pushed Moses to replicate himself as a leader, to delegate his role to others, and to trust that God would use that process (see Exodus 18). Moses had to learn that he had limits. Therefore, one of his key responsibilities was to empower other leaders to lead well in their roles.

We are familiar with the failure-after-success story. A great innovator enters the church with seemingly unlimited energy and charisma. People flock to him. (It's almost always a he—perhaps women are better at resisting or avoiding innovation's temptations and traps.) The church swells with people, confidence, resources, and visions of changing the world. But it all comes to a screeching halt when the visionary leader collapses with a psychological or moral breakdown. The pace of innovation ate him alive. Some of our Edison churches retell this story in their own local contexts. Innovative leaders can undermine the very mission to which they give their lives. Innovation and breakthrough can become the idols they worship.

These are the wrong kinds of failures. These are failures that can crush out new life before it has the chance to establish itself. This is one reason so many innovations and breakthroughs are short-lived. The soil isn't cultivated long enough or deep enough for good roots to take hold. Speed, impatience, moral failure, imbalance, and utilitarianism can all hamper our participation in the work of God. Those with the courage to make change and the passion to seek innovation are sometimes their own greatest enemies in seeing that progress grows lasting roots.

—⁓—

In the kingdom of God, we cannot use people as a means to an end; people *are* the end.

—⁓—

Staying Healthy amidst Innovation

As an innovator familiar with this dark side, Pastor Peter Scazzero explains, "Our greatest weakness flows from our greatest strength. We excel at leading people to a personal relationship with Jesus and mobilizing the church to go out and make disciples of all nations. But because of that excellence, we often do not pay attention to God. We are too active for the kind of reflection needed to sustain a life of love with God and others."[3] Burnout is not part of God's plan for God's children. The pursuit of fruitfulness at the cost of our own physical, emotional, or physical health is not part of God's plan for us. Neither are we to be so dogged in our focus on our mission that we willingly neglect our relationships. How can we bear good news of reconciliation, grace, and redemption if we leave in our wake broken families, lost friendships, and discarded followers?

Two other innovators, JR Woodward and Dan White, warn: "If, for the sake of movement, one sacrifices family on the altar of immediate impact and rapid growth, it often results in the next generation becoming tragically lost."[4]

Dan White Jr.'s book *Subterranean* stands as a prophetic diagnosis and prescription for much that ails churches that seek innovation.[5] According to White, we pioneers can easily become entranced by our own innovations. We can become overly attached to our models and strategies to build the church, to manufacture growth, to create the next new thing that will make all the difference. According to White's diagnosis, all church leaders face several key temptations, especially when trying to innovate.

- We face the trap of *popularity*. In an age of talking heads, often the best talkers become heads and hubs of our organizations. But this cult of impressiveness eventually proves hollow.
- We face the trap of *information*. We think that if we can learn the right things, then we will do the right things, and our churches will be reborn. But the practice of the imitation of Jesus is infinitely more powerful than the cult of information.
- We face the trap of *speed*. We want results, and we want them quickly. "We allow our fixes to be led around by the numbers leash. We are twisting and turning under the strain of numbers."[6] Innovation is an uneven process. Sometimes the hardest work is the deconstruction before the rebuilding can begin. Traditional measurements and timelines don't fit innovation well.

"Our ingenuity, intelligent ideas, and cutting-edge approaches cannot replace the soul's craving being rooted," White summarizes. "We can build churches higher to the sky and host worship events that explode in stadium-size emotion, but the missional future of the church needs a deep reflection on and recovery of its roots."[7] Instead, White argues that the kingdom is more like a tree that we cultivate than a shiny hotel that we manufacture. What the church needs most is not high-end leaders who will innovate new strategies or build new church systems. What the church needs most is deep roots in the kingdom values of faithfulness, incarnation, and community.

When we think of innovation in the church, we are growing trees, not corn. Harvest comes in terms of decades, not months. Kingdom cultivation takes places primarily through the long, slow process of discipling people to actually live like Jesus—loving the least and the lost around us. Words and ideas and leaders matter deeply, but far more important is simple, faithful love.

We wrote this book to encourage a new generation of leaders to claim their role in pioneering new life for the kingdom of God. We want to inspire leaders to plant seeds of grace, fail with gusto, and trust God for the results. But we want to encourage all leaders to do so while following the way of Jesus. Without a courageous movement of leaders who are willing to fail, the church in North America will not experience revival or renewal. Without learning to live in the ways of Christ, however, our failures will be all the wrong ones.

Be brave. Trust that, no matter how much you desire to see new life break forth for the kingdom, God wants it even more. Remember that speed kills. Don't sacrifice people on the altar of success. Passionately pursue the your own health, the health of your family, and the health of your church. Trust that this mustard seed of the gospel will, through patient tending and the grace of God, grow into the largest tree in the garden, where lost birds will take shelter in its branches (see Mark 4:30–32).

14

Reflections from a Seasoned Leader

By Dr. Jesse Middendorf

UP TO THIS POINT, we have not highlighted the primary authors of each chapter because we have shared our suggestions generously with one another in the editing process. However, because of Dr. Middendorf's unique history and experience, we would like to pause here near the end to hear his voice of reflection on these stories of innovation.

Dr. Middendorf pastored five churches over a period of twenty-eight years. He also served as a district superintendent and a general superintendent for the Church of the Nazarene for a total of seventeen years. After supposedly retiring, he founded and continues to lead the Center for Pastoral Leadership at Nazarene Theological Seminary in Kansas City, Missouri.

Dr. Middendorf is able to speak to the church from a deep well of personal experience and from a breadth of perspective that few others share. In this chapter, he shares his reflections on the connections between our Edison churches and the important lessons that churches, pastors, and denominational leaders can learn from these local innovators.

Trinity (San Gabriel Valley, California)

I found this to be a very compelling story. Trinity's experience is counter to that of many churches' efforts to become multicultural, multilingual, and multi-site churches. It is intriguing to reflect on the background of the church, beginning with the singular focus as a Chinese church but becoming the diverse church they are today.

The first ingredient that must be considered in this context is the fact that the church is led by a multicultural couple, one of whom is Chinese in heritage. It is not surprising that a church would choose a pastor with a cultural match to the history of that church. The fact that this pastor's wife is Korean was likely a step toward a new paradigm from the very time that they signed on as the new pastoral family to this congregation. Another key factor in the growth and development of this congregation is the intentionality with which they worked to reach into their own community, recognizing the diversity already around them. Hiring a Hispanic associate pastor visibly demonstrated their desire to reflect a genuinely diverse character in the leadership of the church.

It is instructive that the pastor and staff acknowledge that the work of creating and maintaining a multicultural church requires a great deal of careful planning, communication, and patience. You cannot be colorblind and be successful in an endeavor like this. Sometimes people assume that, to create a multicultural church, they must ignore cultural differences in favor of a homogenization of their diversity. In reality, multicultural ministries must be willing to honor the differences inherent in each culture, while developing the skill to work through the differences toward a greater mission together.

It is hard to imagine a more challenging situation than Trinity is navigating. They are multilingual, multicultural, and multisite—yet they seem to be managing it all with a sense of mission and fulfillment.

Westbury (Houston, Texas)

I read this chapter immediately after the Refuge story and found the juxtaposition fascinating. The contrast is stark, but both church settings reflect an intentional and persistent willingness to stop, think, pray, listen, and examine carefully what was needed in their place of ministry. As one might imagine, the outcome for each of these two congregations was remarkably different, but some of the same foundational steps were taken to discern the leadership of the Holy Spirit and the methods that were most appropriate for their setting.

Westbury's story could be superimposed over the life and experience of many of the once thriving churches across America that are located in rapidly changing communities. While Westbury was fortunate to have opened itself to racial diversity in the 1970s, it obviously faced a far different kind of community in 2005. Therefore, the church would need to become radically open to a new approach to becoming a thriving, missionally focused congregation once again.

It is significant that the church had the support of wise denominational leadership, who were willing to help the church do the hard work of making changes to reach out to their community. But that leadership also had the active and willing engagement of a pastor and congregational leadership who were willing to think with open minds, to become vulnerable to the tensions that significant change would bring, and to dedicate the necessary resources in the beginning stages of their journey. It is also obvious that the careful dependence on the Holy Spirit demonstrated by the staff was a vital aspect of this turnaround church. Hannah carried the labor forward with patient listening to the people and to God.

The development of the FAM endeavor has required constant effort and attention over the long haul to achieve community participation and engagement. That kind of patient and deliberate engagement is often difficult for congregations. The missional expectation is often too short term, leading to the abandonment of some projects before the results that were likely on the horizon could be reaped. This church experience should provide hope for many churches in the U.S., but it must also be a cautionary tale. If you are going to be effective in community engagement, you must set your mind to staying at it as long as is necessary to create a new and greater future for the people in the community. The mission of God requires both passion and patience for church and community transformation to be accomplished.

Duneland (Chesterton, Indiana)

The story of Duneland should give hope to churches everywhere. A long-term, traditional church that is perhaps on the verge of closing and yet, if the people tenaciously seek a way to fulfill the dream of God, this church can become home to gracious innovation and renewal. But renewal always comes with a cost, and sometimes the cost seems to include the death of the vision that initially seemed so near at hand. Persistent people, suffering deep grief and loss, can see a new day, but a new day requires the risk-taking steps and courageous efforts that test our resolve to the very depths.

Edison churches not only accept the challenge of thinking outside the box, but they also pay the price—in time, prayer, relationship building, and innovation. Slowly, they build the capacity to become what they have dreamed.

Duneland has gone from an isolated, discouraged, and defeated church to a church that is literally touching the globe in missional engagement. Evangelism flows from vision, growth follows passion, and grace poured out becomes the fuel for a bright future!

St. Thomas Crookes (Sheffield, England)

This profile is filled with lessons that are both positive and negative. It is remarkable that a renewal that began with such fervor and fruitfulness could so painfully implode. One lesson to begin with is cautionary. Even the most Spirit-anointed movement can be destroyed by a lack of genuine and intentional leadership accountability. It is perhaps more remarkable that, after such a collapse, an ongoing ministry would survive, bear fruit, and become a source of effective leadership development for others.

The concept of high accountability and low control bears careful consideration as well. Moving from the rigorous institutional traditions of Anglicanism into a more autonomous existence as a somewhat independent church has borne fruit in this case. Denominational structures are not normally so willing to allow that kind of freedom. It may be that the soil from which such effectiveness grows must be a loosely turned soil. It is worth exploring the ways a denomination might encourage the kind of low control and high accountability that gave Sheffield its impetus for creative and effective engagement in its communities.

Leonardtown (Leonardtown, Maryland)

The initial impression of the Leonardtown church is *tradition*. Situated on the town square, immediately across the street from a city park, one block from the county courthouse, in a typical church building in every sense of the word, you would expect a traditional approach to ministry, defined and somewhat constrained by the facility. What you find instead is a vibrancy, a community engagement, and a missional mindset that contradicts every surface-level appearance. Leonardtown has begun a revitalization that the church has embraced. Where once there was serious question as to whether the congregation would even survive, there is now a thriving faith community of young families who more closely reflect the community's demographics.

A pastor with the courage to return to a church facing an uncertain future and a leadership team of laypeople who had tenaciously held on for more than ten years of turmoil together found a way to challenge "the way we do things." They opened the church up to a variety of community-oriented innovations. With the wisdom to seek the face of God from the beginning, the congregation became more than merely a church on the corner. They became a fixture in the community. In the space of five years, the entire complexion of the church and its relationship to Leonardtown was radically altered, and the result has been amazing. The journey was hard, sometimes frightening, and often overwhelming, but the people set out with an intentionality that would not be deterred.

We authors have often thought that this may be the most encouraging story for many of our readers because the innovations and methods of the Leonardtown church are so accessible. They simply learned to love their neighbors. Persistence, creativity, courage, sacrificial love, and spiritual fervor became the primary resources for this church's turnaround. There is work yet to be done, but the future is secured in the commitment to be there, on that corner, with a passionate dedication to mission.

Sunnyvale (Sunnyvale, California)

Sunnyvale's story is proof that a district structure can indeed be flexible and open enough to allow for the out-of-the-box methods of creative church engagement in the surrounding culture. Some readers may feel unsettled by this project's fluidity, ambiguity, and seeming lack of measurable missional impact. Yet this may well be one of the most important aspects of the model. Millennial young adults are finding meaningful —and, in many cases, strategically important—ways of becoming reengaged with the church of Jesus Christ. That is rare enough to justify paying attention.

The first part of Sunnyvale's story is one of thousands that could be told across North America in every denomination. A large building that housed a thriving and vibrant congregation during the 1970s and 1980s is no guarantee of a viable future for a local church. The willingness of a congregation and a district to join their hearts and minds in seeking an alternative approach to mission gives this story an unusual twist. There are many possible parallels in other locations.

In addition to creative leadership, another critical element for the success of Sunnyvale is the patience of both district and local leaders, especially in the early stages of such a creative experiment. It is striking to read the ambiguity that seemed to characterize the early stages of the Possibility Project. The necessity of creating a different way of measuring the effectiveness of the project required lots of conversation, lots of experimentation, and, no doubt, lots of persuasion of people who were accustomed to the normal metrics that indicate success or failure.

The willingness to fail is also a critical factor in the development of this project. Institutional measures do not often make room for bold experiments. Many other Nazarene districts may be able to model the Northern California district's use of the Sunnyvale endowment for missional development, benefiting both existing congregations as well as providing means for interns who actively seek to take the church into the marketplace and the communities in the Bay Area. Doing so will require rethinking the old paradigms, and it will need the careful, creative engagement of a wide range of generations for it to take root. The organic church, the house church, and the traditional congregation are not destined for conflict. It is far more likely that the institutional church structure must be the catalyst for more creative and diverse approaches to rebirthing the church in a skeptical world.

Scum of the Earth (Denver, Colorado)

Fruitful and effective ministries draw attention. Sometimes, in the very nature of success, effectiveness and fruitfulness can be lost in the fog of acceptance and affirmation. Scum of the Earth is a wonderful example of the necessity of keeping a unique and targeted ministry unique and targeted. This ministry would not be for the faint of heart. In fact, the very makeup of the community that Scum has reached would be frightening to most churches.

Perhaps the most difficult reality for ministries like this is that, if you are going to reach into the brokenness that is the focus of Scum of the Earth, a high tolerance for ambiguity is necessary. That kind of tolerance runs counter to most evangelical churches, especially those within the Holiness tradition. But the necessary ambiguity is not a vagueness of theology or mission. Those are the solid foundation on which the ministry must stand. But effectiveness in this mission requires a radical acceptance of the most rejected people in our world. I thought it particularly poignant that the pastor himself had to practice developing the capacity to accept people as they were when they came. Engaging people in conversation without reference to how they present themselves is not easy for most Christians. We can, however, accept what we do not approve in order to reach those who are most in need of grace and the gospel.

Scum of the Earth Church is the epitome of what we are talking about as an Edison church. It is engaged in a ministry that—to most people—would be awkward at best, repulsive at worst. But it is effectively engaged in bringing the gospel to bear in ways that are obviously transforming people most churches will never see or reach.

Refuge (Durham, North Carolina)

I found myself engaging in reflection on several levels as I read this chapter. In many ways, this chapter opens a door into the often obscure world of a house church. For decades, people have talked about house churches, yet there seems to be little real definition of what that implies, how it functions, and where it intends to go. Refuge faces a question common to many house churches—whether meeting in homes is merely a transitional stage toward a more formal building. It is difficult for many people who have only experienced worship as related to a place, a uniquely designed building, to imagine why that should not be the pattern for the experience we call church. This chapter provides an altogether different paradigm for how a church forms, how it functions, and why house churches might be an authentic and long-term alternative to more traditional forms.

The Refuge story should be valuable for many people, including denominational and judicatory leaders. In much of the world outside the U.S., the concept of a house church is not only viable, but homes are also the only safe and affordable spaces available. Refuge provides a model for kingdom expansion not otherwise available in many places, and perhaps among many populations. This model also offers many intriguing benefits that appeal to millennials. Denominational and judicatory leaders should consider the house church a viable option for denominational support, and one that will require some different measures for accountability.

Eden (Portland, Oregon)

In many ways the beginnings of the vision to plant a new church are somewhat familiar. A faithful and persistent congregation, led by a pastor with a vision for a new generation, work together to find the mind of God for their vision. The depth of the commitment of Portland First Church is remarkable and commendable, however. It was a risky venture, and the pastor and people must have known that. But it was also a Spirit-led vision, and the local church leadership took the task to heart. The measure of the commitment to the vision was vividly and graciously expressed through their giving $200,000 to fund the first two years of ministry for a new, parent-affiliated congregation. While this approach is not unheard of, it is seldom as deeply embraced as it was by Portland First. The willingness to employ the leader of the new ministry as a member of their own staff, and the unfettered access they gave that pastor to plumb their congregation for missionaries to the new community, are both amazing.

Perhaps most significant, though, was the willingness of the parent church to allow the new congregation to form its own identity and strategic plan. This could have been a stifling relationship, as it has proved to be in some other cases. However, with strong and gentle pastoral leadership from the parent church, Eden Community was freed to form its ministries, its worship styles, and its approaches to service and outreach in ways that were consistent with Eden's own mission.

The strengths of the Eden model are found in the intentional design of their service as worship. They will garner further support and credibility in the community as they show up consistently to serve alongside others who are effectively providing ministries and services that Eden Community could never afford to initiate on their own and have no reason to duplicate. The creative design of the worship time and space is reflective of the generational culture to which they are called. While it will not be seen as traditional in many of its approaches, Eden Community certainly reinterprets Christian traditions for the millennial generation to which they are drawn.

The lack of a consistent location for worship gatherings could have been a liability early on. However, the leaders turned this seeming weakness into an opportunity to demonstrate the *going* of the congregation, rather than the *gathering* that seems to characterize so many existing churches. By the time they were able to locate in Hope Chinese Charter School, the die had been cast. Their life as a church on mission had been established, and the location seems now to be a point from which they go in service. What may seem like instability to the casual observer proved to be a strategically defined stability of mission, and this makes the church a vibrant expression of the contemporary body of Christ.

Church in Action (Frankfurt, Germany)

As I read the profile of Church in Action, I found myself in a place of both consternation and delight: consternation that the organic model of church (of which CIA is a quintessential demonstration) is on the surface so chaotic as to be immeasurable and unmanageable, and delight that I found myself thinking of possible locations for launching the same kind of immeasurable, unmanageable ministry in large cities across the U.S. and Canada.

I have personally met the Zimmermanns and have been fascinated by their energy, their entrepreneurial spirit, and their deep commitment to following Christ authentically and missionally. They come from a family that has instilled in them this creative, out-of-the-box, Christocentric view of how the church should function.

Denominational leaders will likely find this model disconcerting. Metrics are hard to come by, and supervision seems fluid and out of reach. But Church in Action is likely a vision of the future in a rapidly changing world where the Christian church is on the outside of the consciousness of the world.

A summary of their model, which should define a missional vision anywhere, is: "Don't try to bring life to the church. Take the church to life." That sounds suspiciously incarnational to me. And it seems to mirror the very life and ministry of Jesus. This model may not be for everyone, but it is a model we cannot and should not ignore.

—◠◡◠—

These congregations are not intended to be patterns for others to mimic or copy.

—◠◡◠—

Don't Try This at Home

As we have examined and reflected on these Edison churches, we have discovered both the benefits and risks of innovation. The benefits are obvious, in that each of the churches examined has made a remarkable kingdom impact in their communities. The pastors and their people have had the courage to ask the hard questions, to think and plan missionally, and to run the risk of failure in attempting to move beyond mere survival or easily defined metrics.

These congregations are not intended to be patterns for others to mimic or copy, however. They are remarkable examples of tenacious commitment to the mission of the church and of the willingness of pastors and people to join hands and hearts in finding ways to move into a new future that was not readily seen or understood. These are churches that found their mission in their communities and worked until they made a genuine impact on the lives of the people around them.

This book is not a how-to book. This is a don't-try-this-at-home book. Don't do what they did. Instead, find what God would have *you* do! Work at it, run the risk of failure, then recover, and keep working at it until the dream of God and the vision of the church come together to make a difference in the lives of people in your context. A holy God has given the best that God had to give, in order to reconcile a broken and alienated world to God's self. It is up to the church, then, in all its forms and methods, to become agents of that reconciliation. Innovation is not the mission. The mission is the transformation of broken people into the holy people of God. Go, therefore . . .

—⁂—

Innovation is not the mission. The mission is the transformation of broken people into the holy people of God.

—⁂—

15

Cultivating More Edison Churches

WHERE DO WE GO from here? What can we learn from these beautiful stories of innovation? What are some of the next steps we can take to begin innovating in our own local contexts? How can we cultivate more Edison churches? As we conclude our journey through the innovation cycles of ten different churches, we want to share some of the lessons we've learned through our time speaking with and learning from these churches.

1. **All innovations are unique.** Perhaps what has impressed us the most as we have written and read these collected stories is the sheer diversity of innovations. Some innovations are small and internal, like Christine Hung's curriculum-free Bible study at Trinity. Other innovations establish a fundamental identity for a church—like Scum of the Earth Church. In Edison churches, all sorts of innovations may emerge.

2. **Faithful innovation is driven by mission.** No Edison church decides to innovate *just* to be different or to try something new. These are not changes for the sake of change. All of these innovations are fueled by a deep passion to help our local churches so

faithfully embody the life and love of Jesus that people all around are drawn to God's grace. Mission drives innovation—not the other way around.

3. **Desperation is the soil of innovation.** Many of our churches made their most dramatic shifts when their very survival was in question. In others, visionary leaders became so frustrated with the existing modes of church that they helped start something completely new. The common link is that most people don't innovate when everything is working just fine. The pain of staying the same must become greater than the pain of trying something new.

4. **Innovation is hyper-local.** All of these churches have a deep passion for their local communities. Eden Community was birthed with a missionary impulse to reach Portland. Trinity radically changed their church ethos to become more welcoming to their neighbors of other cultures. Leonardtown developed a passion for the people gathering literally in their front yard. When churches innovate well, they usually start in their own neighborhoods.

5. **Innovators must be missionaries.** Church in Action reminds us that we church-folk usually don't understand the cultures found in our local bars and other settings that are radically disconnected from the church. If we want to embody the gospel in ways that will make sense to these neighbors, we need to take the posture of learners first. We must move slowly, learning the language, values, and ethos of the people we are trying to reach. We have to incarnate the gospel differently into each new context.

6. **Edison churches tend toward multiculturalism.** We have tried to highlight this fact in the demographics section at the beginning of each chapter. Duneland is the most homogeneous church in this book, but it is still slightly more diverse than its surrounding community. In most cases, one direct result of innovation is increased diversity. Sometimes, as with Westbury, new levels of diversity spur innovation. Nonetheless, as our society globalizes, local contexts diversify. We expect that, as we move forward, all our churches will need to lean more into diversity.

7. **Sustaining innovation requires leadership multiplication.** Innovation that has staying power will transfer from one leader to another. Deeply innovative churches cultivate new leaders and empower them to carry forward the process with more innovations of their own. St. Thomas beautifully demonstrates that in-

novation brings about long-term change when it carries forward into the third and fourth generations of leaders. This requires a steep time investment by the key leaders, but without it, the innovation stalls or implodes.

8. **Traditional metrics are inadequate.** Sunnyvale is a stark reminder that innovative churches cannot be measured by the ABCs: attendance, buildings, and cash. In most cases, those numbers are what economists call lagging indicators. Often, the key innovations happen long before the attendance goes up. Sometimes, the key innovations just don't fit on our charts. How do you measure Cris Zimmermann's two years of quietly learning pub culture before starting a worship service? Furthermore, as our churches experiment with new modes of being church and doing ministry, many of their experiments will not work. They may learn heaps of important lessons, but there won't be measurable results.

9. **Innovators need both flexibility and support.** Innovation is open-ended. We don't always know what our experiments are going to become. When Refuge started as a missional small group, they didn't know they were going to become a fully functioning church. Portland First gave Eden Community the freedom to become whatever they felt they needed to be to reach the unchurched in Portland. The Northern California district and the German district have given Sunnyvale and Church in Action wide latitude to innovate outside the traditional systems while also bringing helpful support structures alongside them.

10. **Innovation may break taboos.** New people are always a little uncomfortable with Duneland's partnership with Free the Girls. Is it okay to talk about bras in church? Church in Action regularly sends teams into brothels. For Scum of the Earth, extreme (perhaps even vulgar) tattoos and piercings are commonplace, and they regularly welcome people from the LGBT community. After the Orlando nightclub massacre in 2016, Trinity's associate pastor, Johnny, delivered flowers to a gay nightclub in their own community. If we want to reach people outside the traditional church box, we have to let the church live outside the box.

11. **Conflict, failure, and pain always accompany innovation.** Pioneering is hard. Even when Leonardtown hired a pastor specifically to help them innovate, he still faced internal resistance.

Duneland has experienced seasons of pruning, when people left because they didn't like the pace or direction of change. Pastor Albert Hung openly discusses how Trinity tries to calibrate the change process to help all their members feel loved and stay engaged. If it hurts, that might be because you're doing it right. Peter Findlay, a pastor at St. Thomas, shares a great insight: "You gain consent at your church twice: first, when you share your new vision (but they aren't expecting it to change things very much); then, you need a second bout of consent when people actually realize that things are going to change." Pace the changes according to the capacity of your people—but expect some difficulty regardless.

12. **Innovation requires patience and perseverance.** Like Edison's thousands of attempts at a viable light bulb, innovation in churches doesn't come easily. We earn each step of progress through trial and error, through prayer and discernment. Like orchard farmers, we are in this for the long haul. We are growing trees, not corn. The seeds we are planting may take decades to fully mature. As pioneers in new lands, innovators know that we have taken up a hard task. We set our hands to the plow, knowing this will probably take longer than we expect.

13. **Innovators don't have to be special.** Some innovators, like the Zimmermanns, are stereotypical entrepreneurs. Others, like Paul MacPherson, are seasoned pastors who finally found the right mixture of desperation and opportunity to try something new. Similarly, Edison churches come in all shapes and sizes. Sheffield is massive, and Sunnyvale is tiny. Leonardtown and Westbury are fairly traditional, while Eden Community and Duneland blend ancient liturgical practices with new expressions of worship and community life. Some innovative churches are new plants like Refuge that were innovative from day one. Others are much older churches like Trinity that found new ways to thrive missionally. We aren't looking for heroic leaders or hipster churches. Any ordinary leader can help guide innovation in any ordinary church. The real key is cultivating an environment where innovation can happen. Missional creativity is birthed among humility, desperation, openness, hunger, and grace.

—ɰ—

Mission drives innovation— not the other way around.

—ɰ—

Our world is hungry—spiritually, relationally, intellectually, and sometimes physically. Our world is trying to satisfy this hunger through all sorts of ineffective and destructive means. God has given the church the DNA to meet our world's deepest hungers, but this DNA often lies latent, unused, and unengaged in churches that are shriveling up. That's the bad news.

What our world needs most is Christians who will confess that what we have been doing is not working well. What our world needs most is Christians who will dream new dreams for the church. What our world needs most is innovators who will lead us stumbling forward into the twenty-first century and beyond. What our world needs most is churches who will allow God to help them be born again.

On one hand, innovation is really hard. It takes years and lots of pain. On the other hand, anyone can do it. Any church can do it. We just need to be open to God's radical grace leading us forward in the Spirit into new ways of being Jesus in our neighborhoods. We can do this because God wants it more than we do! That's the really, really good news.

About the Authors and Acknowledgments

Dr. Jesse Middendorf has been preaching in the Church of the Nazarene since he was sixteen years old. He has served as a pastor, district superintendent, general superintendent, and in so-called retirement as executive director of the Center for Pastoral Leadership at Nazarene Theological Seminary in Kansas City, Missouri. He holds a bachelor's degree from Trevecca Nazarene University, a master's of divinity and doctorate of ministry from Nazarene Theological Seminary, and an honorary doctorate of divinity from Southern Nazarene University. In 2017 he celebrated fifty-five years in ministry and fifty-three years of marriage to Susan.

Jesse would like to thank the pastor and congregation at Leonardtown for graciously opening their church to his probing questions and for giving helpful and candid answers. Jesse would also like to thank Susan for her unfailing support throughout half a century of ministry.

Rev. Megan M. Pardue is the pastor of Refuge, a church-type mission of the Church of the Nazarene. She's a graduate of Southern Nazarene University and Duke Divinity School. In addition to pastoring, she enjoys training preachers in the department of homiletics at Duke Divinity School. She lives in Durham, North Carolina, with her husband, Keith, and their two children.

Megan would like to express her gratitude to Eden Community, Trinity, and Westbury for their willingness to share their experiences and failures and for allowing her the privilege of sharing their stories with others. She also wants to thank her church family at Refuge for the space to explore different expressions of church and community and for their faithfulness to Christ and one another. Most of all, she wants to thank her kids for making her laugh and her husband, Keith, for his unending support, encouragement, and love.

Rev. Greg Arthur is the senior pastor of Duneland Community Church of the Nazarene in Chesterton, Indiana. Following his time at Wheaton College and Denver Seminary, he served churches in Denver, Colorado, and Chapel Hill, North Carolina. In addition to pastoring, Greg serves as the board president of Free the Girls, a nonprofit that provides jobs for survivors of sex trafficking around the globe, and A Little Charity, which supports missionary work through job development in Mozambique. The joys of Greg's life are his wife, Gretchen, and their two children.

Greg would like to thank the people of Duneland for being kingdom pioneers with him. He would also like to express appreciation to the people of St. Thomas and Scum of the Earth for sharing their innovations with the world. Greg lives each day with a heart filled with gratitude for his parents, George and Cassie Arthur, who taught him to love the church, filled his life with Scripture, and have shown him grace embodied each and every day. The overflow of God's presence in their lives has allowed him to live freely, as only a child privileged in love ever could.

Rev. Josh Broward is the team leader for *Edison Churches*. After nine years as a missionary pastor in South Korea, he served four years as associate pastor at Duneland Community Church of the Nazarene. In October 2017, Josh became the director of missional development for the Church of the Nazarene's Northern California district. He is also privileged to serve on the advisory board for the Center for Pastoral Leadership at Nazarene Theological Seminary. He studied at MidAmerica Nazarene University and Nazarene Theological Seminary, and he is currently pursuing a PhD in organizational leadership at Eastern University. Josh is loving life with his beautiful wife, Sarah, and their two precocious kids, Emma and John David.

Josh would like to thank the people of Duneland for the freedom to experiment inside and outside the church. He is also grateful to the folks at Sunnyvale and Church in Action for sharing their stories of joys and struggles on the journey of innovation. Josh couldn't do any writing or thinking or dreaming nearly as well without the support and warmth that Sarah cultivates, so he counts himself lucky and blessed to call her home.

The entire team would like to express our gratitude to Bruce Nuffer for patiently listening to Josh ramble about writing ideas and for pulling out of that tangled conversation the beautiful seed that became *Edison Churches*. Thanks also to Audra Spiven, Bonnie Perry, and the rest of the team at The Foundry Publishing for bringing these stories of innovation to print. May the Spirit breathe life into these words and fan this type of kingdom creativity into a fire that sweeps the globe.

Notes

Foreword

1. Thomas L. Friedman, *Thank You for Being Late: An Optimist's Guide to Thriving in the Age of Accelerations* (New York: Farrar, Straus, and Giroux, 2016), Kindle edition.
2. Ibid.
3. Ibid.

Chapter 1

1. Amy C. Edmondson, "Strategies for Learning from Failure," *Harvard Business Review* (April 2011), https://hbr.org/2011/04/strategies-for-learning-from-failure.
2. Bram Warshafsky, "Why We Have 'Failure Parties' Every Month," 5Crowd Blog (October 14, 2014), http://blog.5crowd.com/#ufh-i-28449379-why-we-have-failure-parties-every-month.
3. Jena McGregor, "How Failure Breeds Success," *Bloomberg Businessweek* (July 9, 2006), https://www.bloomberg.com/news/articles/2006-07-09/how-failure-breeds-success.
4. "What Is Fail Detroit?" Fail Detroit. http://www.faildetroit.com/what-is-fail-detroit/.
5. "Fail Faire: where it's ok to talk about failing," About Fail Faire DC, http://failfairedc.com/about/.
6. "About," *Failure*, http://failuremag.com/about.
7. "About," Fail Forward, https://failforward.org/about.
8. Edmondson, "Strategies for Learning from Failure."
9. Baba Shiv, "Why Failure Drives Innovation," *Insights by Stanford Business*, Stanford Graduate School of Business (March 1, 2011), https://www.gsb.stanford.edu/insights/baba-shiv-why-failure-drives-innovation.
10. Alan Murray, "US vs. China: Whose century is it, anyway?" Fortune (October 22, 2015), http://fortune.com/2015/10/22/editors-desk-21st-century-corporation/.
11. "Intro to the Failure Issue: The F Word," Harvard Business Review (April 1, 2011), https://hbr.org/2011/04/intro-to-the-failure-issue-the-f-word.
12. *The Edisonian* Volume 9 (Fall 2012), Rutgers School of Science and Arts.

Chapter 2

1. John Wigger, "The Unexpected Leader," *Christian History* 114 (2015), https://www.christianhistoryinstitute.org/magazine/article/the-unexpected-leader/.
2. Alan Hirsch, *The Forgotten Ways: Reactivating the Missional Church* (Grand Rapids: Brazos Press, 2006), 20.
3. Ibid.
4. Gary Hamel with Bill Breen, *The Future of Management* (Boston: Harvard Business School Press, 2007), 56–7.

5. J. Oswald Sanders, *Spiritual Leadership: A Commitment to Excellence for Every Believer* (Chicago: Moody Publishers, 2007).

Chapter 3

1. "History of Trinity," Trinity Church, https://onetrinitychurch.org/history/.

2. Christine Hung, "Just the Bible: When We Study God's Word Together, No One Leaves Hungry," *The Table*, http://www.thetablemagazine.org/articles/18-stories/28-just-the-bible-when-we-study-god-s-word-together-no-one-leaves-hungry.

Chapter 4

1. Katharine Shilcutt, "Meet the Minister Building Bridges between Refugee Communities in Westbury," *Houstonia* (September 19, 2016; published in October 2016 issue), https://www.houstoniamag.com/articles/2016/9/19/minister-refugee-communities-westbury-hannah-terry-bayoughraphy-october-2016.

2. Bob Wells, "Westbury UMC's Apartment Ministry Has Helped Resettled Refugees—and the Congregation—Find New Life in Houston," *Faith and Leadership*, https://www.faithandleadership.com/westbury-umcs-apartment-ministry-has-helped-resettled-refugees-and-congregation-find-new-life.

3. Ibid.

4. Ibid.

5. Ibid.

6. Wells, "Westbury UMC's Apartment Ministry."

7. Ibid.

8. Intentional Christian community is broadly defined as a group of people choosing to live in close proximity to one another, often the same residence, complex, or neighborhood, in order to practice their faith together. Such practices often include meeting daily for prayer, sharing meals, and serving together.

The Christian Community Development Association (CCDA) was founded on the three pillars of relocation, redistribution, and reconciliation. Read more about CCDA on their website, ccda.org.

9. Mark R. Gornik, "A New Song on the Streets of Baltimore," *Faith and Leadership* (May 5, 2015), https://www.faithandleadership.com/mark-r-gornik-new-song-streets-baltimore.

10. Hannah Terry, "Coming into View: Apartment Ministry in Southwest Fondren," *Together* (July & August 2012).

11. Hannah Terry, "Can Any Church Do This?" *Faith and Leadership* (April 5, 2016), https://www.faithandleadership.com/hannah-terry-can-any-church-do.

12. Ibid.

13. Wells, "Westbury UMC's Apartment Ministry."

14. Ibid.

15. For more information on the Fondren intentional Christian community and the practices that guided them, see "Rule of Life of the Fondren Apartment Ministry Intentional Community," *Faith and Leadership* (April 5, 2016), https://www.faithandleadership.com/rule-life-fondren-apartment-ministry-intentional-community.

16. Wells, "Westbury UMC's Apartment Ministry."

17. Shilcutt, "Meet the Minister Building Bridges."

18. "Responding to Racism: Westbury UMC Dialogues with the Community," Texas Annual Conference United Methodist Church (August 11, 2016), http://www.txcumc.org/newsdetail/responding-to-racism-westbury-umc-dialogues-with-the-community-5601669.

19. http://www.centerhealingracism.org/.

20. "Responding to Racism."

21. Ibid.

22. Quote from Hannah Terry in "Deep Listening: Fondren Apartment Ministry," *Faith and Leadership* (April 5, 2016), https://www.faithandleadership.com/deep-listening-fondren-apartment-ministry.

23. Terry, "Can Any Church Do This?"

24. Ibid.

25. Elaine A. Heath, "God's People, Gathered, Blessed and Sent Out," *Faith and Leadership* (April 5, 2016), https://www.faithandleadership.com/elaine-heath-gods-people-gathered-blessed-and-sent-out. You can also find out more at missionalwisdom.com.

26. Terry, "Can Any Church Do This?"

27. "Urban + Suburban: Churches Partner in Apartment Ministry," Texas Annual Conference United Methodist Church (April 23, 2015), http://www.txcumc.org/newsdetail/1020138.

Chapter 6

1. Mike Breen, *Building a Discipling Culture* (Pawleys Island, SC: 3D Ministries Publishing, 2011), 5–6.

2. J. Edward Vickers, *Old Sheffield Town: An Historical Miscellany*, 2nd ed. (Sheffield, UK: Hallamshire Press, 1999), 40–59.

3. "UK Christianity 2005–2015," Faith Survey, https://faithsurvey.co.uk/uk-christianity.html.

Chapter 8

1. Derek Sivers, "First Followers: Leadership Lessons from Dancing Guy," February 11, 2010, https://sivers.org/ff.

2. http://www.savingacts.org/mission.

3. http://www.savingacts.org/aboutmedia.

4. James Emery White, *The Rise of the Nones: Understanding and Reaching the Religiously Unaffiliated* (Grand Rapids: Baker Books, 2014).

Chapter 9

1. Young Life is an incarnational, presence-driven youth ministry organization in more than ninety countries. https://www.younglife.org.

Chapter 10

1. Samuel Wells and Marcia A. Owen, *Living without Enemies: Being Present in the Midst of Violence* (Downers Grove, IL: InterVarsity Press, 2011).

2. Marie-Hélène Delval, *Psalms for Young Children* (Grand Rapids: Eerdmans Publishing Company, 2008).

3. An insight from "A Penitential Order: Rite One" from *The Book of Common Prayer*, 1979.

Chapter 11

1. "Rev. Jason Veach," *This Nazarene Life,* produced by Brit Bolerjack. Season 1, Episode 13 (September 12, 2016), http://thisnazlife.com/2016/09/12/ep-13 -rev-jason-veach/.
2. Jason Veach, "Eden Community Ministry Vision Document: 2011–2012."
3. Ibid.
4. "Rev. Jason Veach," *This Nazarene Life.*

Chapter 12

1. Philip Zimmermann, "7 Words That Explain the Missional Church," http://churchinaction.com/7-word-church.
2. Ibid.
3. Ibid.
4. Ibid.
5. Cris Zimmermann, "When God Sends You to California . . . During the Election," http://churchinaction.com/vlog-no-9.
6. "Pastor Eric Smith," *This Nazarene Life,* produced by Brit Bolerjack. Season 1, Episode 12 (August 29, 2016), http://thisnazlife.com/2016/08/29/ep-12-pastor -eric-smith/.
7. Eric Smith, "God Opens the Door . . . to a Pub?" http://churchinaction .com/god-opens-the-door-to-a-pub.
8. "Pastor Eric Smith," *This Nazarene Life.*
9. Ibid.
10. Ibid.
11. Ibid.

Chapter 13

1. "The Quintessential Innovator," *Time* magazine (October 22, 1979), http:// content.time.com/time/magazine/article/0,9171,947523,00.html.
2. Paul Israel, *Edison: A Life of Invention* (Hoboken, NJ: John Wiley & Sons, 2000).
3. Peter Scazzero, *Emotionally Healthy Spirituality: Unleash the Power of Authentic Life in Christ* (Nashville: Thomas Nelson, 2006), 48.
4. JR Woodward and Dan White Jr., *The Church as Movement: Starting and Sustaining Missional-Incarnational Communities* (Downers Grove, IL: IVP Books, 2016), 30.
5. Dan White Jr., *Subterranean: Why the Future of the Church Is Rootedness* (Eugene, OR: Cascade Books, 2015).
6. Ibid., 11.
7. Ibid., 4.